100 GREATEST
HITTERS

Page 1: *Mickey Mantle*
Below: *Barry Bonds*
Bottom left: *George Brett*
Bottom right: *Wade Boggs*
Opposite: *Reggie Jackson*

100
GREATEST
HITTERS

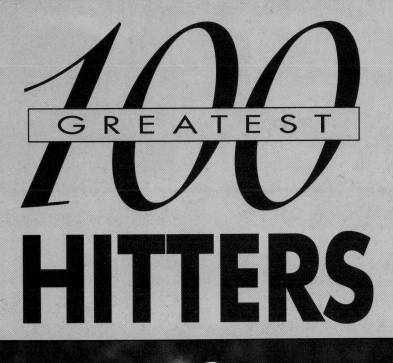

Benton Minks

BARNES
&NOBLE
BOOKS
NEW YORK

Right: *Andre Dawson*
Bottom: *Mel Ott*
Opposite: *George Sisler*

The edition published by
Barnes & Noble, Inc.,
by arrangement with
Brompton Books Corporation

Produced by
Brompton Books Corporation
15 Sherwood Place
Greenwich, CT 06830

ISBN 0-7607-0065-6

Printed in China

Revised and updated 1996

Somewhere amidst the fantasies of everyone who feels passionately about the game of baseball lies the recognition that the nucleus of the game is almost idiotically simple. A player with a modified club stands at a reasonable distance from an opposing player – whose intention is to hurl the ball too fast for the human eye to follow – and tries to make contact with the ball. Baseball purists may proclaim the indispensable attractions of alert baserunning, aggressive fielding and adroit managing (which unquestionably enhance the game's color and intrigue), but the irreducible essence of baseball is pairing off a hitter against a pitcher.

When Charlie Gehringer, Detroit's second baseman in the 1930s, won league honors in nine seasons for best fielding percentage, he courteously acknowledged the recognition, but dismissed his defensive playing as merely something that he had to do in order to get back up to bat. Ted Williams was a reliable outfielder for the Red Sox during his 22 years in Boston, but fans didn't flock to Fenway Park to see him catch fly balls. When Williams was in his rookie season, he unaffectedly broadcast that his singular ambition as a baseball player was to become known as the greatest hitter who ever lived.

This book is a survey that profiles the 100 hitters who, in one person's immodest judgment, qualify as the best in the history of the game. They are arranged alphabetically for convenient reference, but the writer also indulges, perhaps impertinently, in the privilege of ranking them, in a list that appears at the end of the book. There are perhaps 40 to 50 candidates who would make the list of anyone selecting the 100 best, but beyond the first 50 or so, the choosing becomes difficult.

There's no use appealing to 'objective' statistics as the sole criterion, because that's just begging the question. Which statistics are we going to rely on? Do home runs alone a great hitter make? Perhaps the players who've nailed down the top 25-30 places on the all-time home run list deserve automatic inclusion among the select 100. And lifetime average, like home runs, would doubtless gain some other players a place on the list. But soon we'd be wanting to look behind the numbers. Baseball, for all its infatuation with statistics, can't be reduced to cold quantities.

The difficulties are compounded when it comes to selecting active players. Who can know whether a player who has had a great first eight years in the majors won't collapse – next year or during his final eight years? Conversely, what about the young players who may take some years to hit their stride? And then there is the insidious effect of TV, which makes today's players seem so much more impressive than players whom we know only from faded old photographs.

The best 25 or so at the top of this list were those who hit almost at will. They hit not only with uncanny precision, but with enormous force, and dared pitchers to offer their best. The remaining 75 were men who either punished a ball trying to drive it out of a ball park or who hit with such regularity that they tormented pitchers and opposing players. But whatever else may be said of them, all 100 quickened the pulses of fans every time they stepped up to the plate to engage in yet another momentary duel of strength, speed and nerve.

Opposite left: *Ken Griffey, Jr*
Opposite right: *Willie Stargell*
Top left: *Joe Carter*
Top right: *Dave Winfield*
Above: *Robin Yount*
Center: *Tony Gwynn*
Right: *Rod Carew*

Hank Aaron

Henry Louis Aaron

Arguably the greatest home run hitter in baseball history, Hank Aaron never hit more than 47 homers in a single season (1971), but in his 23-year career with the Braves he hit 40 or more eight times, and he averaged more than 33 a year. He hit his 715th to transcend Babe Ruth's record on 8 April 1974 in the fourth inning of a game against the Dodgers in Atlanta Stadium. He was 40 years old at the time, but not yet finished. Playing his last two years with Milwaukee as DH, he tallied 22 more home runs to finish with a lifetime 755.

His slugging was so spectacular that his batting performance otherwise is often overlooked. In ten of his first 12 years he batted over .300, with a high of .355 in 1959. In all he surpassed the .300 mark 14 times. In addition to his home run crown, he holds first place in the major leagues for total games played, times at bat and runs batted in. He ranks third in total hits, second in runs scored, and sixth in the doubles column.

Remarkably durable and consistent, he never had a single year when he dominated hitting, but he assembled a lengthy list of hitting accomplishments and regularly finished among the best in at least one hitting category. Four times, for example, he led the league in slugging percentage, runs batted in, doubles and homers. Twice he was first in hits and twice he won the National League batting title (1956, with .328, and 1959 with .355).

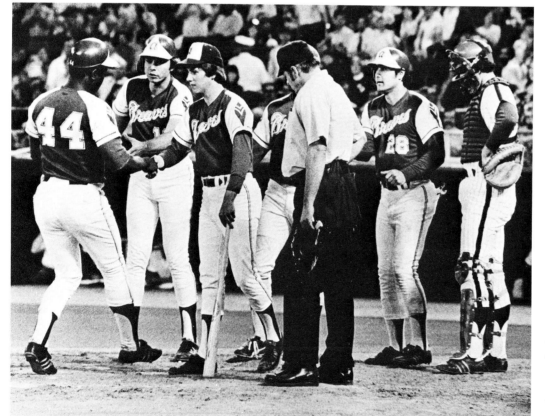

Above: *Hammerin' Hank watches his record-breaking 715th career homer sail out of his home ballpark, 8 April 1974.*

Left: *Aaron (44) gets handshakes from teammates for his 723rd home run against Philadelphia, 4 June 1974, as Phillie catcher Bob Boone looks down.*

Opposite top: *Richie 'Crash' Allen turned in an MVP season in 1972.*

Opposite bottom: *Old-timer Cap Anson of the Chicago White Stockings. The controversial player/manager hit over .300 for 20 years.*

Richie Allen

Richard Anthony Allen

Nicknamed 'Crash' because he hit home runs harder and farther than anyone else from the mid 1960s through 1975, Richie Allen began playing for the Phillies as an 18-year-old in 1960 after declining over 100 college scholarship offers. When he learned that the Phillies were paying weaker players more than the $60,000 they had awarded him, he didn't hesitate to point out that baseball functioned with two standards and that being black was still a disadvantage.

Nevertheless he was Rookie of the Year in the National League in 1964, and he won MVP in the American League eight years later. Twice he was the leading slugger in the American League, and once he led the senior league in total bases. He played for the Phillies the year they won their division, but never played on a pennant-winning team. Unhappy with his undisciplined habits and concluding that he was finished as a player at the age of 30, Los Angeles (for whom he played one year) traded him to the White Sox in 1972. He responded by leading the league with 37 homers, hitting .308 and driving in 113 runs in an MVP performance.

Cap 'Pop' Anson

Adrian Constantine Anson

It would be difficult to name a more lionized baseball hero before the turn of the century than Adrian 'Pop' Anson. His influence on the game as a manager was pervasive in his own time, and it extends up to the present. Spring training, pitcher rotation and the hit-and-run were among his strategies which have since become standard practice.

He signed with the Chicago White Stockings in 1876, and for 20 of his 22 seasons with them he batted over .300. At 6'2" and 200 pounds he had the physical wherewithal to hit the dead ball for distance as well as average. In 1884 he hit five home runs in two consecutive games, all the more remarkable since it occurred at a time when 25 homers a season was spectacular.

A renowned showman, Anson entertained crowds with his merciless vituperation directed at umpires, a performance that delighted fans. His antics were not always so entertaining, however; he took the lead in keeping black players from participating in the major leagues, and his high-handed methods of discrimination were endemic to the game until 1947.

Luke 'Old Aches and Pains' Appling

Lucius Benjamin Appling

Rival pitchers dreaded Luke Appling's coming to bat. Not because he was a home run threat, but because of his uncommon tenacity at the plate. Instead of risking a called third strike in a two-strike count, he would repeatedly foul-off as many as 10 or 12 pitches until he got the one he wanted. And the consistency with which he hit those two-strike pitches was enough to jangle the nerves of the most stoic hurlers.

He holds two records – one accomplished as a result of his superlative hitting, and the other despite that hitting. In 1935 he won the first of two league batting titles with a .388 average (the other, in 1943, with .328), this century's highest for a shortstop. But that level of productivity was not enough to energize an otherwise lifeless White Sox team, which never finished higher than second place in the 20 years (his entire career) Appling was there. That was the longest drought for any player in baseball history.

During that 20-year span Appling played 15 complete seasons and batted over .300 13 times. His lifetime .310 ranks third behind Honus Wagner and Arky Vaughn for shortstops in this century.

Home Run Baker

John Franklin Baker

Home Run Baker's slugging reputation derived more from the number of doubles and triples he hit than from his home run totals (313 doubles, 103 triples and 93 home runs). He did lead the American League in home runs for four successive years (1911-14), with nine, 10, 12 and eight, at a time when home runs often did not go over the fence.

His nickname was actually given to him as a result of two homers that he hit in the 1911 World Series. Baker was playing third base for Connie Mack's Philadelphia As, and in the second game of the Series against the Giants, who were justly proud of having two of the best pitchers in history (Christy Mathewson and Rube Marquard), Home Run hit a homer off Marquard which helped the As win 3-1. Afterward, Mathewson accused his teammate of carelessness with Baker. The next day Baker hit one off Mathewson in the ninth inning to tie the game, which the As won in the eleventh. Marquard responded with his own counter-charge.

During his best home run seasons he averaged .334, .347, .336 and .319 in hitting; and twice (1912, 1913) his RBI totals of 133 and 126 were best in the league.

Above: *Shortstop Luke Appling played for the Chicago White Sox for 20 years (1930-50) and posted a .310 lifetime average.*

Left: *Frank Baker led the league in home runs from 1911-14 as a player for the Philadelphia Athletics.*

Opposite: *Don Baylor.*

Ernie Banks

Ernest Banks

Ernie Banks played all 19 of his years as shortstop with the Chicago Cubs, and in only two complete seasons did he hit .300 or better. His lifetime average was an unspectacular .274

Banks' durable reputation as an all-time leading hitter rests on his unassailable accomplishments as a home run hitter. He hit a total of 512, with 40 or more during five seasons, and he claimed the league home run crown two of those five. His high, in 1958, was 47, an all-time league record for shortstops.

Unimposing in size and manner, Banks attributed his power in hitting to the strength of his wrists. He stroked the ball fluidly but savagely, often connecting for line-drives beyond the reach of infielders.

Although he was predominantly a home run hitter, he led the league once in slugging and was the first National League shortstop since Honus Wagner to lead in RBIs, a title he won two years. He was the first National League player to win consecutive MVP awards (1958 and 1959).

The Cubs were never pennant contenders while Banks was playing: the closest they came was 1969, the year they lost to a fast-closing Mets team. Consequently, Ernie Banks never played in a World Series.

Right: *Chicago Cub shortstop Ernie Banks is greeted at home after nailing his 400th career home run, 2 August 1965.*

Opposite top: *Banks steps into a hit against the Mets, 1962. Hall of Famer Banks' uniform has been retired.*

Don Baylor

Don Edward Baylor

When Don Baylor came to the Red Sox from the Yankees in 1986, he brought along with him more than a reputation for hitting the ball long and hard: He promised a combativeness and an attitude that would not tolerate mediocrity from himself or anyone else on the team. Within his first few weeks in Boston his demand for discipline and excellence from both himself and his teammates was making a difference. A Red Sox team that had been chosen in pre-season to finish in the second half of its division vaulted into first place early and never did fade.

Baylor's playing was among the best in his 16-year career, with 31 home runs and 94 RBIs. Only one other season was better, 1979 with the Angels, when he hit 36 homers, scored 120 runs, drove in 139 and hammered the ball for a .530 slugging percentage – a performance that won him league MVP.

When a moribund Red Sox team traded Baylor to Minnesota (still in contention for its division title) at the end of August in 1987, Dewey Evans, Boston's award-winning rightfielder, predicted that Minnesota would probably win its division title. The Twins won not only their division, but the World Series as well.

In his final year in the majors, 1988, Baylor played only 92 games for the A's. His lifetime 338 home runs and career slugging average of .436 place him among the hitters that opposing pitchers and managers were glad to see retire.

Johnny Bench

Johnny Lee Bench

Describing the position of catcher as so mentally fatiguing that he felt more exhausted after nine innings as catcher than after a week as first baseman, Johnny Bench hit .309 in 1981, his highest average (lifetime: .267). He established himself as a hitter of prominence, however, during his tenure at Cincinnati, when the Reds were perennial contenders, winning six divisional championships, four pennants and two Series.

Named Rookie of the Year in 1968 after his first full season at Cincinnati, he was voted National League MVP two years later when he led the league with 45 home runs and 148 RBIs and became the first catcher in major league history to win both home run and RBI crowns. Two years later he won the MVP again by

driving in 125 runs and belting 40 homers to top the league in both categories. Bench played his whole career with the Reds (1967-83).

A tenacious and explosive competitor, he often won games in late innings with clutch hitting and was always intimidating when he stood at the plate. In the strike-shortened 1972 season Pittsburgh's superior pitching assured it the favored position in the play-offs with Cincinnati, but in the fifth and decisive game Bench tied the game with a home run in the ninth inning, and the Reds eventually won.

Yogi Berra

Lawrence Peter Berra

He never won a home run, RBI or batting title, but his hitting always won as much respect for him as any other part of his game. He came to the Yankees the year Bill Dickey retired (1946), and he sustained the Yankee legacy of premier catching for the better part of two decades. In all but three of Yogi's 17 full years with the Yankees the team won at least the pennant.

Berra's hitting contributed mightily to Yankee strength during those dynastic years. For ten consecutive seasons (1949-58) he hit over 20 home runs and reached 30 twice. Five times he drove in more than 100 runs – 125 in 1954. One of the best hitters of the time to come into a tight spot, particularly late in a game, he would often reach out and hit a pitch far outside the strike zone and drive it out of reach of the infield or even over the wall. He rarely struck out – in 1950 just 12 times in 597 times at bat.

His best season as a hitter was 1950, when he batted .322, hit 28 home runs and drove in 124 runs. He hit 12 homers in a total of 75 World Series games, and he had more times at bat, more hits and more doubles than any other player in World Series competition.

Below: *Yogi Berra belts a three-run homer.*

Above: *Clutch-hitter Johnny Bench, National League MVP in 1970 and 1972.*

Wade Boggs

Wade Anthony Boggs

Wade Boggs had as inauspicious a beginning as anyone can imagine when he first played as a back-up first/ third baseman in 1982, the year he joined the Red Sox. Regular third baseman Carney Lansford, league batting champion, had injured his ankle on 24 June trying to stretch a long triple into a home run, and Boggs was thrust into the game. Boggs raised his batting average from .211 to .370 within the first month, and he ended the season hitting .349. Yet he didn't qualify for the batting crown because manager Ralph Houk benched him when Lansford returned after six weeks.

In the next season Boggs won the first of a string of league batting titles; from 1983 to 1987 he took the title four times (his average in 1987 was .363). 1987 was also his fifth consecutive year with 200 or more hits, a mark he shares with Charlie Gehringer, Chuck Klein, Al Simmons and Wee Willie Keeler.

In 1993 Red Sox faithful assumed the team had made another mistake by trading Boggs to the Yankees, but the mistake has not materialized. Since his last season

Above: *Bosox star of the 1980s Wade Boggs became a Yankee in 1993.*

Bottom: *Barry Bonds has made his mark with the Pirates and the Giants.*

in Boston (.259) his pace has dropped by more than 20 points by lifetime standards, but even in those years he hit over .300. Bothered by a bad back in 1996, he nonetheless helped the Yankees win the World Series.

Barry Bonds

Barry Bonds

Scan the columns for batting leaders from 1986 to 1995 and one name comes up as often as any of the others for the NL. Barry Bonds had the most runs (109) in 1992; most home runs in 1993 (46); most RBIs in 1993 (123); and was best in slugging percentage in both 1992 and 1993 (.624 and .677). Lest anyone question his impact on the league thus far in the 1990s, he has been chosen MVP twice, in 1992 and 1993.

Bonds has played on only one championship team thus far in his eleven years. He began his career in Pittsburgh in 1986 and played in the LCS against Cincinnati in 1990. Cincinnati won and Bonds had an abysmal series, going 3 for 16 and driving in only one run. He joined the Giants in 1993 and proceeded to hit 43 homers, collect 123 RBIs and lead the league in slugging with .677.

He has averaged more than 30 home runs a season in his first eleven years, enough to place him in the top ten among active players. He is in the top five in slugging average for players with at least 2000 hits; and his on-base percentage was best in the league three consecutive years, 1991-93.

For the 1996 season he was fourth in the league in

slugging, third in runs scored, and second in on-base percentage, and his 42 homers were second best in the league. Even though his career may be half over, Bonds could become one of the titans of hitting in baseball by the turn of the century. And before he sets new lifetime records, he just may play for a world champion.

Jim 'Sunny Jim' Bottomley

James LeRoy Bottomley

One of the first products of a minor-league feeder system for major-league competition, Jim Bottomley began his professional baseball career playing for the Sioux City team of the Western League in 1920. On 18 August 1922 he played his first game in the major leagues, when the Cardinals called on him in a game against the Phillies. The game went 14 innings, and Bottomley managed one hit in 17 at-bats. By the end of that season, however, he was averaging .325 for 37 games and was playing first base for St Louis full time.

His first complete season, 1923, was sensational, with a .371 average in 134 games, second in the league to Rogers Hornsby. Although his hitting performance that year was his lifetime best, he nonetheless hit over .300 in nine of his first 10 years in the majors and had a lifetime .310. The only time during that 10-year stretch he hit below .300 (.299), he led the league with 120 RBIs and 40 doubles.

Twice he hit six for six, the most memorable time being on 16 September 1924, when his six hits included a grand-slam homer in the fourth inning and a two-run homer in the sixth.

Left: *Jim Bottomley of the Cardinals batted in 12 runs with six hits in one game in 1924.*

Opposite top: *George Brett, a Kansas City Royal his entire career, gets set to round the bases after launching a home run.*

Opposite bottom: *Brett is surrounded by Royals teammates at home plate. In 1985, the veteran slugger had a .335 hitting average, with 30 home runs, 112 RBIs and 38 doubles.*

George Brett

George Howard Brett

By the end of the 1987 season, George Brett had a .290 batting average, with 78 RBIs and 22 home runs – a disheartening season for a masterly hitter. Disheartening not because of the home run or RBI count, but the average was that of the player who has come the closest to Ted Williams' benchmark .406 in the last 46 years. Brett had a league-leading .390 in 1980, and he had thus far hit under .300 only five times in his 15 seasons at Kansas City.

1986 was no better – he finished an injury-shortened season hitting .290. But such mediocre hitting did not remain a problem for Brett. Brett insisted that one secret to hitting is convincing yourself that you're in a better position than the pitcher.

Brett carried the Royals to seven division titles, two pennants and one World Championship. Perhaps his most memorable homer was the one he hit against Goose Gossage in game three of the 1980 championship series against the Yankees. Gossage was delivering at 100 mph, but Brett, already winner of the league batting crown, drove in three runs and won the game with a homer in the seventh inning.

The last year he batted over .300 was 1990. Nonetheless, after 21 years, all with the Royals, Brett retired in 1993 with 317 home runs and a lifetime .305 hitting – enough to earn a place among the all-time great hitters.

Jesse 'The Crab' Burkett

Jesse Cail Burkett

Only Ty Cobb and Rogers Hornsby were able to match Jesse Burkett's achievement of three seasons hitting over .400. Attributing his batting to confidence, he asserted at one time that he could hit over .300 just by bunting – not an idle boast, since he had mastered the ability to bunt foul on third-strike pitches until he got a pitch he liked.

His first .400 year was 1895, when he led the National League with .423. Playing for the Cleveland Spiders, he was also first that year in hits, with 235. A year later he led the league in hits (240), runs scored (159), games played (133), at-bats (585) and average (.410).

After the collapse of the Spiders in 1897, Burkett went to the St Louis Cardinals, where he hit .402, his third time over .400, in his first year with them.

While playing for Cleveland he acquired the nickname 'Crab' because his joyless disposition on the field often resulted in his exchanging insults with fans, and occasionally punches with other players.

Right: *Buntmaster Jesse Burkett played for the Cleveland Spiders, St Louis Cardinals and Boston Somersets and thrice hit over .400.*

Opposite: *Roy Campanella, Brooklyn Dodger catcher (1948-57), is greeted by joyous teammates after lambasting a long homer.*

Below: *Campanella crunches a ball during batting practice at Ebbets Field.*

Roy Campanella

Roy Campanella

Roy Campanella began playing baseball for a living at the age of 24, but he played his first three years in the Negro leagues and consequently received no attention. His first year in the major leagues was 1948, when he began playing for the Brooklyn Dodgers.

A giant figure in the pages of Roger Kahn's celebrated *The Boys of Summer*, he was the victim of a destructive car wreck in January of 1958, when he lost control of his car on an icy road and broke his neck. After 10 sensational years he was a paraplegic.

In his second season Campanella was already making a difference for the Dodgers, who won the pennant in 1949 and entered the decade of the 1950s as one of the strongest, most unforgettable teams in National League and baseball history. He had quickly captured attention and respect with 22 homers and a .287 hitting average in that 1949 season. Two years later he raised his hitting performance to 33 home runs, 108 RBIs and a .325 average, for which he was elected MVP. He had two more exceptional years with the Dodgers in Brooklyn (1953 and 1955) winning MVP honors.

Rod Carew

Rodney Klein Carew

Only Honus Wagner (with eight) and Ty Cobb (with 12) have won more batting titles than Rod Carew. Possibly the most consistent hitter in the game during the past two decades, he hit over .300 during 15 consecutive seasons (1969-1984). In 1977 he was the first batter to threaten Ted Williams' .406 record for the American League set in 1941. Rod Carew worked for batting average, not home runs, because he was convinced he could help win more games that way.

He was just beginning to play baseball at the age of 15 when a scout for Minnesota discovered him in New York City. He signed with the Twins in 1964, and after three years with a farm club he began playing in the major leagues in 1967. Two years later (1969) he won his first batting crown, with a .332 average. In 1977 he batted .388 and tied his personal home run best (14),

had 38 doubles, 16 triples, 239 hits and 100 RBIs. Three times he claimed league honors for most hits, and twice for triples. His .388 average for 1977 was the highest since Ted Williams' .388 in 1957, and his total of 239 hits that year almost equaled the record of 254 that Bill Terry had set in 1930.

Jim Palmer's advice about pitching to Carew was to simply deliver the pitch and then pray that he would hit it someplace where someone could field it.

Below: *Rod Carew played for the Twins and Angels and was a consistent and dangerous hitting force. He earned six AL batting titles.*

Opposite top: *Blue Jays power hitter Joe Carter.*

Opposite bottom: *Orlando Cepeda won Rookie of the Year at 20.*

Joe Carter

Joseph Chris Carter

In the early years of the 1990s Toronto added a new wrinkle to major league baseball history by becoming the first non-American team to contend for a post-season title. Joe Carter was a principal player in the Blue Jays' ascendance from everlasting second division to World Champions in two successive years.

Carter started his career in the NL with the Cubs. Then he served six years with Cleveland (1984-89) before spending a season with the Padres. Carter didn't play close to a full season until his second year with the Indians when he hit 15 homers and drove in 59. He nearly doubled those numbers in both categories in 1986 with 29 homers and 121 RBIs; and he was among the leaders in both leagues in homers and RBIs, averaging 30 HRs and 110 RBIs every year through 1994.

Only 15 years into his career he has amassed hitting totals which place him among the leaders for active players, many of whom have played years longer. Through 1996 he ranked in the top five in lifetime home runs and RBIs and was among the top 20 in doubles, total runs and total hits.

Carter's most storied single stroke was the blast that detonated the Phillies' hopes in 1993 for their first World Series win in ten years. Joe Carter's three-run drive silenced volumes of skepticism as the Blue Jays won their second straight world title.

Orlando 'The Baby Bull, 'Cha-Cha' Cepeda

Orlando Manuel Cepeda

Incapacitated by knee injuries almost at the time he had begun to define himself as a hitter and slugger of the first rank, Orlando Cepeda nevertheless hit a career total of 379 home runs, and he tied Tony Perez for 26th place in the top 50 honor roll for lifetime home runs in the major leagues. He began playing for San Francisco as a 20-year-old and achieved Rookie of the Year with a .312 average. After the age of 25, however, he was able to put together only two more exceptional seasons.

In one of these, 1967, when he was with St Louis, he hit .325, with 25 homers and 111 RBIs, to win MVP over his closest rival Roberto Clemente, in a unanimous vote by the 20-member committee.

His first six years were a rush of achievement; in his fourth season (1961) he hit 46 homers, drove in 142 runs and averaged .311. By the time he was 26 he was averaging almost 32 home runs a season, his RBI average was over 100 per year and he batted under .300 only once. His hitting pace at that time was ahead of Hank Aaron's, also a 20-year-old rookie. He continued playing until 1974, despite injuries, and he finished with a lifetime .297 average.

Will 'The Thrill' Clark

William Nuschler Clark

San Francisco last played in a World Series in 1989, when Will Clark was finishing his fourth season in the major leagues (all with the Giants). Clark's hitting for the series was uncharacteristically mediocre: only 4 hits in 16 at-bats and only one for extra bases, a double. Without Clark's hitting throughout the season, though, the Giants probably would not have been in the Series at all. 1989 was one of those specimen years that San Francisco, and Clark, would refer back to as a standard. He played in all but three games for the season, had 196 hits (only Tony Gwynn had more, at 203) and scored 104 runs (the league's best). Seventy of his 196 hits were for extra bases (fourth best in the NL). His on-base percentage was .407, third best in the NL, and he ranked second in the league in total bases.

The World Series year was not Clark's only standout season: the year before (1988) he tallied 29 home runs and won the NL RBI title with 109. He smashed 29 homers again in 1991, the year he won the league title for slugging percentage with a .536. His best homer year was 1987, when he finished with 35 – in addition to 29 doubles and 5 triples he stroked while

cruising along at a .308 average for the season.

Clark moved to Texas in 1994. In his first two seasons with the Rangers he averaged just under .300 hitting and 15 home runs, below his customary numbers; but in 1996 he helped Texas win its first spot in postseason play in team history.

Roberto Clemente

Roberto Walker Clemente

Even without his baseball heroics, Roberto Clemente would occupy a niche in the pantheon of exceptional people in recent history as a result of the relief mission he undertook to assist the victims of the devastating Nicaraguan earthquake in December 1972. During that mission he was killed in a plane crash.

His death was a severe loss to baseball, as well as to his friends and family and to his lifelong team, the Pittsburgh Pirates. Only a few months before the disaster, in the season's last game, he had become the first Puerto Rican player (and the eleventh player in league history) to connect for his 3000th hit, when he rifled a double against the Mets in Shea Stadium. In 1971 he had resurrected the drowsy Pirates from a two-game deficit to win the World Series against the Orioles. He was named the Series MVP, batting .414.

A premier hitter, he averaged over .300 13 of his 18 seasons and finished with a lifetime .317. Four times he won the batting title, recording his best year in 1967 with an enviable .357. Twice more he hit over .350 (.351 in 1961 and .352 in 1970) and in his last three years averaged .352, .341 and .312 respectively.

Above: *Roberto Clemente of Pittsburgh connects for his 3000th hit September 1972.*

Top: *Will Clark helped the Giants to the World Series in 1989. In 1994 he went to the Rangers.*

Ty 'The Georgia Peach' Cobb

Tyrus Raymond Cobb

Above: *Ty Cobb slides. The feisty Georgian won 12 batting titles and batted over .300 in 23 seasons.*

Ty Cobb's hitting records are so transcendent that they appear almost fictional. In 24 seasons he accumulated a staggering total of 4191 hits (the most for any hitter in history until Pete Rose hit number 4192 in September 1985). Though not regarded as a slugger, his 723 lifetime doubles rank him third in the major leagues. He holds second place for triples, with 297. He scored the most runs in history, and he is fourth in RBIs behind Hank Aaron, Babe Ruth and Lou Gehrig. Above all, his lifetime average of .367 seems one of those records that may last forever.

Nine consecutive years (1907-15) he was the league leader in batting. Three of those years, 1911-13, he hit an astounding .420, .410 and .390. His last three batting titles came in 1917, 1918 and 1919, when he hit .383, .382 and .384 respectively. Three years later he went over .400 again, with .401. He batted over .300 every season except his first – 23 in all. He held the record of nine seasons with 200 hits until Pete Rose broke it in 1979.

After 1920 he was forced to yield in popularity to Babe Ruth, despite a .356 hitting average during his last nine years of playing. At 40 years of age he hit .357, and his final year (1928) he hit .323. Although Ruth captivated fans with his spectacular slugging, Cobb surpassed even the Babe in one statistic when he smashed five homers in two successive games on 5 and 6 May 1925. He hit only 12 that entire year, but he finished with a .378 average.

There is so much more that could be said about this incredible player if space permitted, but for our purposes the stats will have to be enough. Even to add that he was one of baseball's true greats would be fatuous.

Mickey 'Black Mike' Cochrane

Gordon Stanley Cochrane

Mickey Cochrane still holds the best lifetime hitting average for catchers in the major leagues, .320. Black Mike didn't begin playing until he was 22 years old. An excellent student as well as an exceptional athlete, he attended Boston University after graduating from high school. After two years in the minors, he signed with Connie Mack's As and didn't waste any time adjusting.

His first year, 1925, he batted .331, and in nine years with Philadelphia he was a decisive factor in the team's winning three pennants. In those winning years he hit .331, .357 and .349. He often batted first or second because of his extraordinary speed. When Cochrane was followed by Jimmie Foxx and Al Simmons in the line-up, the combination presented as deadly a hitting trio as any in the game's history.

In need of cash, Connie Mack sold Mickey to the Tigers in 1934 for $100,000. At the age of 31 the new catcher-manager proceeded to win pennants in his first two years in Detroit, and in 1935 he led the Tigers to the team's first World Series victory. Yankee pitcher Bump Hadley nearly killed him in May 1937 with a beanball. Mickey finished that season as manager, but he was unable ever to play again.

Right: *The Philadelphia As won three pennants during lethal lead-hitter Mickey Cochrane's tenure.*

Opposite top: *Eddie Collins entered the Hall of Fame in 1939 with a career .333 hitting average.*

Opposite bottom: *Collins unwinds after a pre-game hit.*

Eddie 'Cocky' Collins

Edward Trowbridge Collins, Sr

One of Eddie Collins' most distinguished records is the 25 continuous years he played in the American League. He began at the age of 19, hitting only .235 with the Philadelphia As. After a 12-year span with the White Sox, he returned to Philadelphia for his last four years. When he retired at the age of 43, he had a lifetime .333 average.

In all but seven of his 25 seasons he batted over .300, his best year being 1920, when he hit .369. Although he never won a batting title, his 3311 hits rank him third best in the league and seventh best in major league history.

He never hit more than six home runs in a season, but he was a master at driving the ball through the infield to get on base and then using his speed and intelligence to advance. Three times he led the league in runs scored.

Collins played in six World Series (34 games) and hit at an average of .324. One of the Series in which he didn't play was the one in 1920. The White Sox were favorites to take their second straight pennant that year, but many of the team's big names were suspended when the scandal of the 1919 Series surfaced. Happily for baseball, Eddie Collins was among the few White Sox players uncorrupted by the scheme.

Andre 'Hawk' Dawson

Andre Nolan Dawson

In his first ten years (1977-86) Andre Dawson batted .346 at Chicago's Wrigley Field – but he was playing for Montreal. In 1987 he moved over to join the Cubs, but ironically he did not hit that well in the Cubs' home park. Nevertheless, he ended the 1987 season with some fine over-all stats: .287 batting average, 137 RBIs, and 49 home runs – the last figure good enough to earn him first-place standing in his league.

Respected for his speed as well as for his hitting (a few years ago Dawson's fellow major leaguers voted him the best all-around player), Dawson was National League Rookie of the Year in 1977. When he left the Expos he was batting .280 and averaging almost 23 home runs a season. He was the league MVP in 1987.

Dawson batted in the American League for the first time in 1993 when he played for Boston through the strike-shortened 1994 season. Not surprisingly he maintained his status as a clutch long-ball hitter with the second highest homer tally for the Sox in 1993-94. The Hawk retired in 1996 with a home run tally of 438, enough to keep him among the all-time leaders.

Opposite: *Andre Dawson was the first member of a last-place team to be named MVP in 1987, his first year with the Cubs.*

Left: *Dawson was the 1977 NL Rookie of the Year with the Expos.*

Below: *Big Ed Delahanty was a true slugger, known for long, hard hits.*

Ed 'Big Ed' Delahanty

Edward James Delahanty

The only player to win batting championships in both the National and American Leagues was Ed Delahanty. Big Ed stands fourth in the all-time list of lifetime hitting averages, with a .346.

He became a major-leaguer in 1888 at the age of 20, when he began playing for the Phillies. He did not reach .300 until 1892, when he hit .313 and led the league in doubles, with 33. His first sensational season was the next year, 1893, when he hammered 19 home runs (only five other players in major league history had hit more up until then) and finished the year with a .371 average. In 1894 he completed his first of two .400 seasons: His .408 in 1899 led the league.

His long-ball hitting began to draw crowds. On one occasion he ripped a worn ball in two, and on another he took out a pitcher who was expecting a bunt but instead got a line-drive that smashed his ankle. On 13 July 1896 he hit four home runs in a single game – only the second player to accomplish such a performance. Ed's slugging reputation, alas, was almost matched by his notoriety for immoderate drinking and brawling. He fell off a train, apparently while drunk, and his body was eventually found below Niagara Falls.

Joe 'Joltin' Joe,' 'The Yankee Clipper' DiMaggio

Joseph Paul DiMaggio

The player who probably represented the strongest challenge to Ted Williams' supremacy in hitting in the 1940s was Joe DiMaggio. When Williams entered the major leagues, DiMaggio was playing in his fourth year and had just won his first of three MVPs after hitting .381. In his first four years he had a combined average of .343.

Joe was a consummate baseball player, not just a superlative hitter, but his batting provided some of the most memorable moments in baseball history. His record of hitting in 56 consecutive games still stands. That legendary achievement began in May 1941, when he hit one for four against the White Sox. It did not end until 17 July, when, playing in Cleveland, he was denied a hit twice by the brilliant fielding of third baseman Ken Keltner. In that same season he struck out only 13 times in 541 at-bats and averaged .357 in hitting, drove in 125 runs and belted out 30 homers.

His 1949 heroics have remained one of baseball's best stories. Returning in June after recurring pain from a bone spur on his right heel sidelined him in the spring, Joe hit four homers and drove in nine runs as the Yankees won three games from Boston to remain in contention for the pennant. He played in 76 games that season, hitting .346 and driving in 67 runs – and the Yankees won the pennant.

Cecil Fielder

Cecil Grant Fielder

Cecil Fielder had one of the worst years in his career in 1995. He hit 31 home runs and drove in 82 runs. Thirty-one home runs would be a more than respectable performance for ordinary mortals who labor to achieve the two-figure mark for any of the extra-base categories in a season. For Fielder, though, such numbers are just not good enough.

Touting a chop swing reminiscent of that of the great Babe Ruth, he hit with punishing and explosive force from 1990 through 1993. With the upper-body mass and strength of a heavyweight in the ring, Fielder inspired slack-jawed amazement with regularity as he would fire a howitzer 480-plus feet into the second tier of Tiger Stadium. In one memorable contest with the White Sox Fielder and Frank Thomas carried on their own home run derby. By game's end both had incited pandemonium by crushing three homers of the tape-measure variety.

Fielder led the league in home runs with 51 in 1990 and 44 in 1991. He was first in slugging in 1990 (.592) and won the RBI title three successive years (1990-92) with 132, 133 and 124 totals respectively.

Moving to the Yankees after mid-season in 1996,

Cecil wielded his big bat to help the Pinstripes win their first World Series since 1981.

Opposite: *Legendary Joltin' Joe DiMaggio hit 361 home runs.*

Right: *Cecil Fielder led the majors in RBIs from 1990 through 1992.*

Jimmie 'Double X,' 'The Beast' Foxx

James Emory Foxx

An unforgettable moment in the fictional story of Roy Hobbs, hero of Bernard Malamud's *The Natural*, occurs when Hobbs hits the ball so hard the cover comes off. Jimmie Foxx was that kind of hitter in real life. More than one account credited him with hitting the ball with such force that it would lose its shape. His lowest home run production for a period of 12 years (1929-40) was 30, in 1931. A disappointing year for him, yet he batted in 120 runs and hit .291.

He hit 534 homers in his 20 years of playing – modest perhaps by the standards of Ruth and Aaron, but fans considered him in the same class with Ruth, and after Babe retired, Foxx long reigned as the dominant home run hitter in the league.

Winner of four home run titles (one a tie) and three RBI crowns, he was always dangerous at the plate, even when not pasting the ball. In 1938, his third year with the Red Sox, he batted .349, in addition to hitting 50 homers and driving in 175 runs, his highest. The following year, when Williams was a rookie, he improved his average to .360 and finished with a lifetime average of .325 in 1945.

Frankie 'The Fordham Flash' Frisch

Frank Francis Frisch

Frankie Frisch came to St Louis in 1927, batting .335 after seven full years with the Giants. It was an otherwise unheralded move, except he was replacing the best hitter in National League history, Rogers Hornsby.

Cardinal fans were at first incensed by the loss of Hornsby, but the Fordham Flash proved in his first year that the trade was to the Cardinals' advantage. He came to St Louis with sound credentials, having played for the Giants in four consecutive pennant-winning seasons, during which he hit .351, .327, .348 and .328. He batted over .300 for 11 straight seasons (13 altogether), and he finished with a .316 lifetime average. Although he 'never went for a home run when a single would win a game,' Frisch is considered the first power-hitting switch hitter in the major leagues.

Possibly his most shining moment occurred in the 1934 World Series, when he helped the Gashouse Gang win the seventh game against Detroit. Detroit manager Mickey Cochran had walked the batter before Frisch, plotting a double-play. Frisch, however, fouled off four pitches and then drove in two runs with a searing double to right field. With that example to inspire them the Cardinals scored five more times in that inning and eventually won 11-0.

Opposite: *Jimmie Foxx was a terror at the plate, often knocking the leather off and shape out of the ball. His lifetime statistics include 534 home runs and a .325 hitting average.*

Right: *It wasn't long before switch-hitter Frankie Frisch stepped out of Rogers Hornsby's shadow and into the hearts of St Louis Cardinals fans.*

Lou 'The Iron Horse' Gehrig

Henry Louis Gehrig

Frank Graham of the *New York Sun* memorialized Lou Gehrig's first appearance in Yankee Stadium. During batting practice Gehrig unknowingly picked up Babe Ruth's bat and missed on his first two swings before bouncing one over second base. The next time up he hit one into the same distant zone where only Ruth had hit them. Then he hit three more into the same territory, while the rest of the team looked on, speechless.

The Iron Horse not only batted in tandem with Babe Ruth, he was and is among the few power-hitters belonging in the same rank as the Babe. The year Ruth hit his 60 homers Gehrig hit 47, had 175 RBIs (11 more than Ruth) and averaged .373 (Ruth was .356).

His lifetime average of .340 ranks him among the top ten in the majors, but other numbers are even more impressive. Seven times he drove in over 150 runs per season. He hit more than 40 doubles seven times, and eight times 10 or more triples. He averaged over .340 eight times. He hit 23 grand-slam homers, still a major league record. And in 34 World Series games he hit 10 home runs, batted in 35 runs and averaged .361.

A desperately sick man, on 1 May 1939 he removed himself from the line-up, and on 4 July of that year he closed his career with the immortal farewell line in which he called himself 'the luckiest man on the face of the earth.' Two years later, not quite 38, he died.

Charlie Gehringer

Charles Leonard Gehringer

Called 'The Mechanical Man', Charlie Gehringer was not a hitter who felt threatened by a two-strike count. He preferred, in fact, not even to swing until the pitcher had two strikes on him, insisting that it concentrated his mind wonderfully. There must have been some truth to this, since he usually ended with a line drive instead of striking out. In 19 seasons he had more than 30 strike-outs only three times.

A second baseman for Detroit from 1924 to 1942, he led the league nine times in fielding percentage, but his precision defensive work was not sufficient cause for celebration; it was merely a necessary interlude before he could return to the plate. He led the league in hitting in 1937 (.371), after hitting .354, .330 and .356 respectively in the three previous seasons. From 1927 through 1939 he batted over .300 every season but one, when he hit .298.

He hit 60 doubles in 1936, and in 16 complete seasons he batted in over 100 runs in a season seven times. And seven times he had more than 200 hits. His level-headed consistency is evident in his .321 average in three World Series and a lifetime figure of .320. He became a Hall of Famer in 1949.

Opposite (inset): *Lou Gehrig.*

Opposite: *'The Iron Horse' won the triple crown in 1934.*

Right: *Charlie Gehringer played for the Detroit Tigers. His almost error-free play at second base earned him the nickname 'The Mechanical Man.'*

Josh Gibson

Joshua Gibson

Probably the best known of the old Negro League players after Satchel Paige, Josh Gibson could catch like Roy Campanella and hit like Hank Aaron. Gibson played his first game in the Negro Leagues on 25 July 1930 in Pittsburgh, when Judy Johnson, manager of the Homestead Grays, called him out of the stands to substitute for the regular catcher, who had refused to play because of the bad lighting. (It was the first night game ever played in Forbes Field.) Gibson played the rest of that season and the next, when he hit 75 home runs for the Grays. Then he moved across town to the Pittsburg Crawfords, who got his five most productive years. He rejoined the Grays in 1937 and stayed with them, with two years out for the Mexican League, until his premature death in 1947.

Records for the Negro Leagues are not always authoritative, but Gibson seems to have hit as many as 84 homers in one season, and he is credited with a total of 962 homers, although not all were against league teams. His lifetime average was .391, while his average in exhibition games against major leaguers was .412.

He played frequently in Washington's Griffith Stadium, where Negro League games often attracted more fans than the Senators. Clark Griffith, owner of the Senators, flirted with the thought of signing him, but chose not to face the consequences. Gibson died only a few months before Jackie Robinson took to the field as a Dodger, but Gibson has joined Robinson in the Hall of Fame.

Goose Goslin

Leon Allen Goslin

Goose Goslin played left field for Washington and was a major reason why the Senators became league champions in 1924. It was their first time, and a particularly satisfying triumph for Washington fans, since it prevented a Yankee pennant for a third successive year.

The Senators won the league championship again the next year, and among the elated fans was President Calvin Coolidge, who, along with Mrs. Coolidge, attended three World Series games and presented a trophy to the team, despite their loss to the Giants in seven games.

Goose did not save his best hitting for championship years. He won the batting crown on the last day of the 1928 season by edging Heinie Manush by a single percentage point, and the four previous years (1924-27) he proved he was a legitimate contender with averages of .344, .334, .354 and .334.

Opposite: *Josh Gibson of the Homestead Grays stands poised to bat. Gibson hit 75 homers in his sophomore season in the Negro League.*

Above: *Goose Goslin hits to centerfield in the 1925 World Series against the Pirates. The Senator leftfielder had a .316 career average.*

His best slugging year was 1930, when he hit 37 home runs and drove in 138 runs. In 11 of his first 13 seasons he drove in 100 or more runs per season, and he beat Babe Ruth in 1924, with 129 to Ruth's 121. He entered the Hall of Fame in 1968.

Hank 'Hammerin' Hank' Greenberg

Henry Benjamin Greenberg

In an era of exceptional hitting, featuring such names as Ruth, Gehrig and DiMaggio of the Yankees and Foxx of the As and Red Sox, Detroit's Hank Greenberg compiled a list of personal statistics that compared well with anyone's. He batted over .300 in seven of the nine years in which he played 100 or more games. In four of those seasons he won the home run crown, with a high of 58 in 1938, and he tied for the lead a fifth time. Four times he was first in RBIs, and in 1937 he collected 183 – one shy of Lou Gehrig's all-time league record.

Gehrig's stardom with the Yankees persuaded Greenberg that he would be wise to play for a team other than New York, even though he had grown up in the city and the Yankees had shown an interest in him. Joe DiMaggio was Greenberg's most persistent rival for RBI honors from 1937-41, and Hank considered that his two RBI titles won during those years were a personal triumph.

During his 12 years at Detroit, the Tigers won the pennant four times, and in World Series competition Greenberg batted .318, with five homers and 22 RBIs.

Ken Griffey, Jr

George Kenneth Griffey, Jr

Left: *Hank Greenberg's grand slam home run (11 July 1945) won the pennant for the Tigers.*

Above, above right and below: *Ken Griffey, Jr is considered by many the best player in baseball today.*

On 26 May 1995 Ken Griffey, Jr ran into the centerfield wall with such force while making a dazzling catch that he crushed his left wrist. Just 73 games later the bionic Griffey was vaulting off the same wall after stealing at least a double from another frustrated batter.

More astounding, though, was the quick recovery of his timing and strength at the plate. Even with his damaged wrist at only 80 percent of the force it carried in the spring Griffey was hitting homers again, one unforgettable one coming as a last-pitch game winner against the Yankees in mid-August.

Unquestionably one of the most talented athletes to come along in the last decade, Griffey had already put together some daunting numbers before the injury. By the time he turned 25, he had tallied 1000 hits – only the sixth player in history to reach that plateau at such a youthful age.

With one of the sweetest strokes in the game, 'Junior' delivered his 180th homer within just a few days after his return to the Mariners' line-up. He is the third youngest player to hit the 150 home run mark. The injury presented a momentary disruption in his five successive years of over .300 hitting and two years in a row with 40 or more home runs, but he did hit seven homers in the postseason against the Yankees and the Indians; and in 1996 he batted .307 and added 49 home runs to his rapidly growing total.

Tony Gwynn

Anthony Keith Gwynn

Tony Gwynn's scorching bat was at least one reason fans were so resentful about the aborted 1994 season. When custodians padlocked the last ballpark gate on 11 August, Gwynn was the most promising prospect in years to equal or break Ted Williams' 1941 season hitting average of .406. With 45 games remaining in the regular schedule, the San Diego outfielder was batting .386, with a mere 19 strikeouts in 419 at-bats. His 34 doubles and 12 homers fixed his slugging average at .566; and his on-base and slugging averages combined were sixth best in the majors.

His numbers in 1995 were not quite as transcen-dent, but they were scintillating nonetheless. The .368 hitting he posted for the season was more than 30 points higher than second best in the NL; and only one player in the AL was hitting in the same range (Edgar Martinez for Seattle).

In 15 years playing in the majors, all with San Diego, he stands in first place among active players for BA, and he ranks in the top ten for doubles, triples and runs scored; and in the top five in total hits. He won his seventh batting crown in 1996. His age, 36, would keep him on track for putting up formidable numbers by the end of the 1990s.

Harry 'Slug' Heilmann

Harry Edwin Heilmann

Right: *A protege of Ty Cobb, Harry Heilmann recorded a lifetime .342 batting average.*

Opposite: *Tony Gwynn was in line to break Ted Williams' record 1941 season batting average of .406 when the 1994 season ended prematurely.*

Slug Heilmann didn't catch fire until 1919, his fifth season with Detroit, but during the 1920s he became a volatile hitter, winning the batting title in 1921, 1923, 1925 and 1927 with averages of .394, .403, .393 and .398. Had he managed nine more hits during those years, he would have averaged over .400 four times.

Lest there be any doubt about what he did during the even-numbered years when he wasn't winning the batting crown, he hit .356, .346 and .367. His main competition during the decade of the twenties came from two of the game's hitting giants – George Sisler and Babe Ruth.

A pupil of Ty Cobb, who managed and played some of Heilmann's years in Detroit, Slug averaged .357 for the decade, and during his seven best years (1921-27) he hit .379. His lifetime .342 stands seventh in the major leagues since 1900 for players who played in 1000 or more games.

He was not a home run hitter, but he nonetheless had sufficient power to smash 542 doubles, over 40 in each of eight seasons. And eight times he accumulated more than 100 RBIs and he hit over 200 times per season in four seasons. He entered the Hall of Fame in 1952.

Rickey Henderson

Rickey Henley Henderson

The baserunner who continues to give opposing managers in the American League the most anxiety is Rickey Henderson. In 1985 he led the league in runs scored, with 146, and was the league leader again in 1986, with 130. The 146 were the most runs scored in the majors since the lengthening of the season in the early 1960s. Ted Williams was the last player to score more runs in a single season (150 in 1949). Henderson scored over 100 runs a year in the 1982-86 seasons.

Playing his first six years for Oakland, he hit to get on base so that he could swipe at least one more. In 1985, however, he began emerging as a potent long-ball hitter. While at Oakland he averaged .291 in batting and collected only 51 homers. (His highest home run total, 16, was in 1984.) But in 1985, his first year with the Yankees, he hit 24 homers, and in 1986 he hit 28. His numbers in doubles have risen just as steadily – 27 in 1984, 29 in 1985 and 31 in 1986.

After pulling a hamstring early in the 1987 season, Henderson returned at midseason in 1989 and continued to post respectable numbers in doubles and home runs. In 1990, his first full year back with the A's, he tallied 33 two-baggers, 28 homers and hit at a .325 clip for the year – a performance which helped mightily in the Athletics' sweep of the Red Sox for the pennant. Henderson switched leagues for the first time in 1996 to play for the division champion Padres.

Rogers 'Rajah' Hornsby

Rogers Hornsby

Rogers Hornsby's hitting for the Cardinals in 1920, .370, was good enough to win the league batting title, one of nine he would win, but it was his lowest average in the years through 1925. From 1921 through 1925 his hitting numbers were .397, .401, .384, .424 (still the best in the major leagues) and .403. The three seasons in which he hit over .400 he also averaged 34 home runs. His .358 lifetime average is a close second behind the all-time leader Ty Cobb's .367, and he is still in seventh place for all-time slugging percentage.

Rajah always terrorized pitchers, so much so in his .424 year that his hitting, combined with intentional walks, resulted in a trip to base more than half the times he came to the plate. It is true that he played during a decade of inflated hitting statistics that resulted from a hopped-up ball, but compared to other hitting numbers of the same time, his are still astronomical. In 1922, for example, the entire National League hit .292; Hornsby hit .401, with 42 homers and 154 RBIs.

After spending his first 12 years with St Louis, he played for six different teams during his remaining 11 years. When he was at his peak and full of talent he may have been somewhat lacking in personal grace, but he was the best hitter of his time, even if he was his own most enthusiastic fan.

Opposite: *Rickey Henderson, speedy base-stealer for six years in Oakland, started slugging on his arrival in New York.*

Above: *Rogers Hornsby's .424 batting average in 1924 is still a record.*

Frank 'The Capital Punisher', 'Hondo' Howard

Frank Oliver Howard

At the end of the 1963 season, Frank Howard had played only four years in the major leagues, all with the Dodgers, but he had just batted .300 and had hit one home run in the World Series against the Yankees, a Series the Dodgers swept. Even so, Howard was threatening to retire.

Rookie of the Year in 1960, he had batted .296 and had hit 15 home runs, but disgruntled fans had expected even more from the former Ohio State University .366 hitter. In his second season he batted .296 again, but he more than doubled his home run production, to 31, and drove in 119 runs. Still the fans complained. He asked to be traded, and the Dodgers, after at first refusing, sent him to Washington.

As a Senator he hit some of the longest home runs in major league history, and he was about the only attraction in the team's waning years. In his 1968 season his 44 homers were best in the major leagues, and he set a major league record by hitting 10 of those home runs in only 20 at-bats in six games. Probably the most memorable homer of his 382 lifetime total was at Tiger Stadium in Detroit, where he smashed a Mickey Lolich pitch onto the roof, and eventually outside the stadium itself.

Opposite: *Frank Howard in a Dodger uniform. Failing to satisfy fans in Los Angeles, he delighted Washington with his battery of homers.*

Right: *Joe Jackson hunkers down for a hit in 1919. Jackson went to two World Series with the Chicago White Sox, in 1917 and 1919.*

Joe 'Shoeless Joe' Jackson

Joseph Jefferson Jackson

Shoeless Joe Jackson almost held the distinction of posting the highest hitting average of the century. His .408 at the end of the 1911 season was not high enough to overcome the commanding performance of Ty Cobb, who finished with a .420 average. Jackson was, in fact, the only major league hitter to bat over .390 two years in a row and not win a batting title, also thanks to Cobb.

When Joe was traded by Cleveland to Chicago in 1915, fans at Comiskey Park watched the White Sox quickly become the strongest team in the American

League, and one that promised to be one of the best in baseball history. They won the pennant in 1917 and 1919 and the World Series in 1917. But in 1919 they lost the Series to Cincinnati through chicanery, and Shoeless Joe was among the eight White Sox players charged with plotting to lose the Series.

In his 11 full seasons Jackson averaged over .360 and finished with a lifetime .356, third highest in history behind Cobb's .367 and Hornsby's .358. His home run hitting was never a threat, but his 307 doubles and 168 triples attest to his abilities as a long-ball hitter.

Reggie 'Mr October' Jackson

Reginald Martinez Jackson

Throughout the 1987 season Reggie Jackson gave slightly contradictory signals to baseball fans: He was either going to retire at the end of the season, no matter what, or he was going to remain in baseball until he could hit his 574th home run. As all true followers of the game knew, the significance of the latter goal was to place Jackson one home run ahead of Harmon Killebrew, and thus gain Jackson the fifth rank in career homers, a position he could probably count on lasting for many years to come. In the end, Jackson did announce his retirement, and his 563 homers left him in sixth place on the all-time list of home runs.

The way Jackson managed to keep his career plans in the spotlight was typical, for perhaps more than any other player of the last two decades Jackson managed to keep himself in the headlines, inspiring both adulation and anger by his tactics on and off field. As Mr October he somehow always managed to perform dashingly in the last weeks of the season, often in a championship series or the World Series. In 1977, for instance, when he and the Yankees faced the Dodgers for the second consecutive year in the World Series, Reggie won MVP for the Series after hitting five homers, including three on three successive pitches.

Jackson's career average of .260 may not be all that spectacular. But he will nevertheless go down in baseball history as one of the game's most powerful hitters and memorable personalities.

Below: *Reggie Jackson eyes his third home run in the sixth game of the 1977 World Series against the Dodgers.*

Opposite: *Jackson demonstrates power-hitting and leverage as he wallops the ball against Cleveland, 6 July 1980.*

Judy Johnson

William Julius Johnson

Acknowledged the best third baseman in the Negro Leagues, Judy Johnson played many games in Pittsburgh, where Pie Traynor played for the Pirates, and fans who followed black baseball referred to Johnson as 'the black Pie Traynor.'

After signing his first contract in 1918 for $5 a game, in 1921 Johnson moved to a Philadelphia club, Hilldale. There he improved his salary to $150 each month, enough to buy himself a new glove every year and to own two pairs of shoes – one for good fields and the other for the miry conditions that were then all too common. In the 1920s Connie Mack remarked that Johnson, had he been white, could have named any salary he wanted.

Never a power hitter (usually no more than two or three home runs a year), he was a dangerous line-drive batter with hitting averages usually in the high .300s. In 1924 his .341 was the best hitting in the first Negro World Series. The next year he reached probably his best average, with .392 – while nursing an arm broken during a game early in the season. His lifetime average of .349 won him election to the Hall of Fame in 1975.

Opposite bottom: *Judy Johnson, lethal with his line drives.*

Above: *Detroit Tiger Al Kaline's batting average was .340 in 1955.*

Right: *Kaline helped the Tigers win the 1968 World Series, batting .379.*

Al Kaline

Albert William Kaline

Had he hit one more home run, the Tigers' Al Kaline would have been the first American League player to achieve the distinction of making 3000 lifetime hits, 400 of which would have been homers. He didn't even think about the importance of the mark until five years after he had retired, and Carl Yastrzemski became the first.

His inattentiveness to such details characterized his attitude toward playing – an indifference toward setting personal records but a determination to do whatever he could to help his team win. He admitted that his only incentive for hitting homers was to win a game. In each of two seasons he hit 29, his highest total, even though the Tigers tried to induce him to become more of a slugger.

In 1955, 20 years old and in his second full season, he won the league batting title with a .340 average. It was to be his only title, though he was consistently a contender. He hit over .300 nine times, and only his last two seasons (.255 and .262) reduced his lifetime average to .297.

The year Denny McLain won 31 games (1968), the Tigers won the pennant and Kaline batted .379 to help Detroit beat St Louis in the World Series.

Willie 'Wee Willie' Keeler

William Henry Keeler

From 1892 to 1894 the Baltimore Orioles moved from last place in the old National League to first. One of the reasons for such a dramatic surge was Wee Willie Keeler, who batted .371 in 1894, the year the Orioles began rivalling the Boston Beaneaters for dominance in the league. In the last Temple Cup series ever played, Keeler hit .424 in the five-game championship contest, and Baltimore beat the Beaneaters four games to one.

Keeler was a masterly hitter whose accomplishments are all the more striking when examined within the context of the tactics his teammates applied. Unlike the rest of the team, Keeler would not file his spikes, though spiking, profanity and physically holding baserunners were all part of Baltimore's celebrated strategy for winning. Refusing any cheap tricks, Keeler won games, championships and titles by 'hitting 'em where they ain't.' In 19 years he struck out only 36 times, and in 1897 he set the mark of 40 successive games in which he hit safely. Keeler entered the Hall of Fame in 1939.

Charlie 'King Kong' Keller

Charles Ernest Keller

The same year Ted Williams began in Boston, and served notice of his intentions by hitting .323, another rookie, Charlie 'King Kong' Keller, joined the Yankees and posted an even more assertive .334 average. He did not hit as well again in his relatively brief career in the major leagues, but he did bat over .300 twice more and finished with a lifetime .286. In his first eight years his slugging percentage was over .400. Three times he hit 30 or more home runs in a season, and twice he hit over 20. Three times he batted in over 100 runs, and he batted in 90 or more three other years.

Keller's auspicious rookie performance helped lift the morale of Yankee fans, who were still stunned by the loss of Lou Gehrig. Keller played left field, and with DiMaggio in right field and Tommy Henrich in center, the Yankees regained their position of supremacy in the American League in 1939 and finished with 106 wins, 17 better than the second place Red Sox. In the World Series that year Keller played brilliantly, with a .438 average, three home runs, a triple, a double and six RBIs. But he was the victim of a congenital back disease and was forced to retire in 1952, after only 13 seasons.

Opposite left: *Rather than resort to cheap tactics for victories, Willie Keeler used his philosophy of 'keep your eyes clear and hit 'em where they ain't' to achieve a .345 lifetime batting average.*

Opposite right: *Charlie Keller's .286 career batting average belied his true hitting prowess, for he had 189 lifetime home runs and hit .438 in the 1939 World Series, in which he also had six RBIs.*

Below left: *King Kelly, who played every position while with Chicago (1880-89), chalked up 1820 hits during his career, with a .307 average.*

King Kelly

Michael Joseph Kelly

When the owners of the Boston Nationals paid the Chicago White Stockings $100,000 for the services of Mike 'King' Kelly in 1887, newspaper editors either pontificated about shameless decadence or celebrated Boston's coup: Such was the status of King Kelly, perhaps the first superstar of baseball, who reigned for many years at the end of the nineteenth century.

Kelly had acquired his reputation before he left Chicago, where he played with player-manager Cap Anson. Slightly ribald and certainly rowdy, Kelly was renowned as much for his antics on and off the field as for his playing. One of his improvisations, which became a standard baseball tactic, was to skid under, around or into the defenseman covering a base. This inspired a popular song of the day, 'Slide, Kelly, slide!'

Kelly began with Chicago in 1878, and in his last year with the team he was hitting .388 and scoring 155 runs. He would never again have such a season; indeed, Boston's management tolerated his unruliness for only four years and then sold him to the New York National team in 1893. New York, in turn, sacked him before the season ended. That ended his major league career, but he retired with a respectable .307 career average and 1820 hits. Hardly one of the game's power-hitters, Kelly nevertheless demonstrated that there was more to hitting than home runs.

Harmon 'Killer' Killebrew

Harmon Clayton Killebrew

In 1959 Harmon Killebrew almost single-handedly rekindled enthusiasm for baseball in Washington, a city in which fans had had little reason to cheer for years. He won the home run title that year, with a total of 42. More remarkable was the fact that he became the first home run champion in history to win the crown while hitting below .250, a pattern that remained constant throughout his career. The only season in which he batted over .300, in fact, was his first, when he played in only nine games.

He led the league four times, and he tied for first twice. In 1969 he won MVP, with 140 RBIs and 49 homers, and he helped the Twins win the second of three division titles while he was there. During his first four seasons with Minnesota (1961-64) he roused fans by hitting 46, 48, 45 and 49 homers. The 1965 team was a pennant winner and 'Mister Torso' hit a home run and batted .286 in the World Series against the Dodgers. His 573 career homers rank him fifth in the majors.

Ralph Kiner

Ralph McPherron Kiner

Ralph Kiner played baseball mostly to hit home runs. He played only 10 years, but in that time he hit 369 homers. In his first seven seasons he either led or tied for the lead in home runs in the National League. Over his 10 years he averaged a home run every 14 times he went to the plate, second only to Babe Ruth, whose frequency was one homer for each 11.7 at-bats.

In his rookie year (1946) with Pittsburgh, where he played all but his last three years, he won the home run title in a season when Stan Musial won every other batting title. In his second season he hit 51 and tied Johnny Mize of the Giants for the league title. Alas, he didn't improve the last-place position of the Pirates, but the fans made no secret of their enthusiasm for Kiner's slugging, despite the lustreless play of the rest of the team. They would often pack up and leave after Kiner's last at-bat whenever there was no chance he would come up again.

Never claiming to be a precision or clutch hitter, Kiner averaged .279 lifetime, with three seasons over .300, and he once candidly observed that players who hit for average drive Fords, while home run hitters drive Cadillacs.

Above left: *Harmon Killebrew nails his 537th homer.*

Above: *Pirate Kiner.*

Opposite: *Chuck Klein.*

Chuck Klein

Charles Herbert Klein

1930 was a resounding year for Chuck Klein. In his second full season he posted numbers in all five hitting categories that would have won him titles ordinarily. But his .386 average, his .687 slugging percentage, his 40 home runs, his 170 RBIs and his 250 hits were not enough to give him a single crown. His team, the Phillies, averaged almost six runs per game yet finished last in the league. This was because everybody else was clobbering the ball, which had been enlivened to enhance a game suffering from the trauma of national economic catastrophe.

Klein's next year, 1931, was relatively more modest, with 31 homers, 121 RBIs and a .337 average, but now he led the league in home runs and RBIs and had certified his position as a power hitter in the league. Two years later he batted .368 and was first in the league, with 120 RBIs. He was also first with 28 home runs, and first with 44 doubles and best in hits (223). In all but one of his first 10 seasons he hit .300 or better. And Klein remains the only National League player to accumulate 120 or more RBIs in his first five full seasons. He became a Hall of Famer in 1980.

Ted 'Klu' Kluszewski

Theodore Bernard Kluszewski

'Mr Torso' of the Cincinnati Reds is still recognized as a heavyweight in the slugging fraternity. He played his best years for Cincinnati (1947-57), and throughout the middle fifties admirers regarded him as the most likely contender to break Babe Ruth's home run record. During a four-year span, 1953-56, his home run production was 40, 49, 47 and 35 respectively. In 1956 not only were the Reds a serious threat to the Brooklyn Dodgers' supremacy; Kluszewski teamed with Frank Robinson, Wally Post and Gus Bell to tie the Giants' major-league record for total homers in a season (221).

Klu was able to hit not only for distance, but for average as well. In his relatively short 15-year career he hit over .300 seven times, and he averaged almost .316 during his five peak years (1952-56). His lifetime average is .298. He was an excellent first-baseman as well as a slugger: His lifetime fielding percentage is .993. He was second in voting for Most Valuable Player of the National League in 1954.

Playing for the White Sox against the Dodgers in the 1959 World Series, he hit three home runs and set a new record for RBIs in a six-game Series – six.

Nap 'Larry' Lajoie

Napoleon Lajoie

Nap Lajoie was so preeminent as player-manager of Cleveland from 1905-09 that the team was nicknamed the 'Naps'. One of 111 former National League players to transfer to the fledgling American League in 1901, he dominated the young league's hitting before the advent of Ty Cobb. In his first year in the new league, with the Athletics, he captured the Triple Crown with 14 home runs, 125 RBIs and a .422 average (still a league record).

The rivalry between Lajoie and Ty Cobb was so vigorous that in 1910 Cobb elected not to play in the season's last game in order to protect his slight lead over Lajoie for the batting title. Lajoie lost by a single percentage point (.384 to .385), despite a conspiracy by St Louis Browns' manager and a coach who tried to help Nap's performance in a double-header ending the season. After that Lajoie played seven more years, but manager Jack O'Connon and coach Harry Howell never participated in major league baseball again.

Nap led the league in hitting for the next three years after he won the triple crown (1901), with averages of .378, .355 and .377. He retired in 1916 with 3251 hits and a lifetime .339.

Opposite: *Ted Kluszewski of Cincinnati had a high hitting average, as well as a tendency to slug multiple homers. Fielders never had a clue where the ball was going.*

Right: *A photo-mosaic featuring Napolean Lajoie at bat for the Philadelphia Athletics. Lajoie ended his career in 1916 with 3251 hits and an average of .339.*

Tony 'Poosh 'Em Up' Lazzeri

Anthony Michael Lazzeri

In his rookie year he drove in 114 runs, second only to league leader Babe Ruth. When Tony Lazzeri came to the Yankees from the Pacific League in 1926, he had never even seen a major league game. He played for the Yankees from 1926 to 1937, and in those years he won an enviable reputation for hitting with men on base. Poosh 'Em Up Tony averaged 96 RBIs a year while with the Yankees.

The most unforgettable RBI he did *not* get was in the 1926 World Series between the Yankees and the Cardinals. In the seventh inning of game seven, with the Cards leading 3-2 and the bases loaded for the Yankees, Cardinal Manager Rogers Hornsby feared Lazzeri enough to call in Grover Alexander as relief, even though Alexander had pitched a full game the day before, beating New York 10-2. Lazzeri tagged the second pitch hard enough to drive in at least the tying run, but it was foul. Alexander then struck him out, and the Cardinals won the Series.

In his 14 seasons in the majors Lazzeri hit .300 or over five times (.354 in 1929). He drove in more than 100 runs per season seven times.

Below left: *Tony Lazzeri, New York RBI king.*

Below: *Lazzeri averaged .400 in the 1937 Series.*

Opposite: *Buck Leonard gets set to smash one for the Homestead Grays.*

Buck Leonard

Walter Fenner Leonard

When the first black player, Jackie Robinson, was allowed to participate in major league baseball in 1947, Buck Leonard was already 38 years old. But it was another eight years before Bill Veeck offered him a chance to play with the St Louis Browns. Leonard himself declined, explaining that he felt he wasn't up to the level of major league play at that time.

Buck played for 17 years at first base for the Homestead Grays, a team in Pittsburgh that attracted some of the best black players. With the Grays, he earned a reputation for his fielding as well as his hitting.

Although perhaps not the great home-run hitter that his teammate Josh Gibson was, Leonard hit his share – 42 in 1942. But it was his powerful line drives and his consistency that earned Leonard his place in the Baseball Hall of Fame in 1972.

His 17-year average with the Grays was .341 (in 1947, he ended up with .410), while in exhibition games against major leaguers he averaged .382. In the 11 Black All Star games he appeared in, he averaged .317. The prejudices that kept Buck out of the major leagues during his peak years cost baseball dearly.

Pop Lloyd

John Henry Lloyd

Honus Wagner considered it an honor when fans of Pop Lloyd called him the 'Black Wagner.' Lloyd began playing baseball for a livelihood in 1906, when he became a member of the Cuban X-Giants (with no Cubans on the team) as a 22-year-old. In his first game he hit a double in the tenth inning that won the game and catapulted him into a sensational 25-year hitting career.

In 1907 he tried to improve his prospects and income by going north to Philadelphia, where he played three seasons with the all-black Philadelphia Giants. After the 1910 summer season he played for the Almendares team in Cuba during the winter. (Salaries for black players made no provision for off-season.) In a 12-game exhibition series against Detroit, Lloyd hit .500; Ty Cobb hit .370.

The next year (1911), during one of the rare times anyone bothered compiling records for black players, Lloyd played in New York City, starring with the Lincoln Giants. In 62 games played in Harlem at 136th Street and Fifth Avenue Pop Lloyd had 112 hits for a .476 average. In the years that followed Lloyd moved from team to team, ending up his career in 1931 with a lifetime average of .365. By the time he was taken into the Baseball Hall of Fame he had come to be regarded as one of the greatest baseball players of all time.

Mickey 'The Commerce Comet' Mantle

Mickey Charles Mantle

Occasionally there comes along a batter who hits more than ordinary home runs, a titan who can drive a ball right out of a ball park. Mickey Mantle was one of those.

He nearly did it in Yankee Stadium in 1962, when he drove a ball 600 feet, and his 565-foot measured homer in Griffith Stadium finished in the parking lot. On many occasions he hit line drives off the centerfield wall – 450 feet – in Yankee Stadium. He was equally devastating batting right-handed or left, and he smashed two homers, one right-handed and one left-handed, in 10 separate games, a record no one has matched.

Coming to the Yankees in 1951, DiMaggio's last season, Mantle played 18 years for New York, 12 of which were World Series seasons for the Yankees. In those 12 World Series he set records for home runs (18), runs batted in (40) and runs scored (42). His numbers, apart from championship play, are just as brilliant: Four times home run leader, once in triples, six times best in runs scored and four times in slugging percentage.

In his final season, when he hit .327, he was walked more than 100 times, his tenth 100-plus walk season. His most spectacular season was 1956, when he became the sixth hitter in the American League to win the Triple Crown, with a .353 average, 52 homers and 130 RBIs. His 536 lifetime home run total is seventh on the all-time list.

Opposite top: *John Henry 'Pop' Lloyd posted an incredible .476 hitting average in 1911. The star Negro League player had a career .365 average.*

Left: *New York Yankee Mickey Mantle, in the midst of his classic swing, prepares to blast one out of the stadium in the third game of the 1960 World Series vs Pittsburgh.*

Below: *Diagram depicting Mantle's rocket 565-foot homer (which landed in the parking lot) in Griffith Stadium.*

Roger Maris

Roger Eugene Maris

The second most interesting detail about Roger Maris's batting reputation is usually overlooked: He was a splendid hitter in *addition* to what he accomplished in 1961. In 12 seasons he collected a total of 275 homers, twice he led the league in RBIs and for two consecutive years he was voted league MVP. After hitting his 61 homers in 1961 he finished the next year with 33 and drove in 100 runs for a third successive year.

When Commissioner Ford Frick decided that any home runs hit beyond the 154th game would not be valid as a new record surpassing Babe Ruth's 60, Maris did not relinquish his assault. At 154 games he had 59. In the face of relentless scrutiny, harassment and even threats, he hit number 60 on 26 September, and then, in an historic moment in Yankee Stadium, he hit his 61st on 1 October 1961 in his second at-bat. It was the final day of the season and a real heart-stopper for everyone there.

Maris had no interest in being a public spectacle and said afterward that breaking the record had only made his life more complicated. In his five remaining seasons with the Yankees, while fans jeered as much as cheered him, he concentrated on hitting doubles and singles.

Below: *Yankee Roger Maris connects for his 61st home run of the 1961 season.*

Opposite top: *Milwaukee Braves' third baseman Eddie Mathews pounds the 400th home run of his career in April 1963.*

Opposite bottom: *Yankee first baseman Don Mattingly led the American League in RBIs (145) and doubles (48) in 1985.*

Eddie Mathews

Edwin Lee Mathews

If home run hitting is a standard for measuring hitting performance, Eddie Mathews's qualifications are undeniable. He hit 20 or more in each of 14 consecutive seasons with the Braves, and in four of those his number was 40 or better, enough to win the home run title twice.

For 13 years he followed Hank Aaron in the line-up, and that combination, with 'The Hammer' Aaron batting right-handed and Mathews batting left, produced more homers than any other duo in the history of the game, 60 more than the 1207 Ruth and Gehrig generated when they played together. Mathews and Aaron were instrumental in the Milwaukee Braves' winning pennants in 1957 and 1958.

Mathews was built like a slugger, with an enormous arm and upper-body strength that enabled him to drive some of the longest balls in the history of Milwaukee County Stadium. In his first year at Milwaukee he hit at a .302 pace and slammed 47 homers, easily enough to win him celebrity status among fans. He batted over .300 three times, and though he has a modest lifetime average of .271, he is tied with Ernie Banks for 11th place in all-time home run hitting in the major leagues.

Don Mattingly

Donald Arthur Mattingly

When Don Mattingly hit his third grand-slam home run in less than two months on 11 July 1987 against the White Sox, it was his fourth homer in three games. Four games later he had hit six more home runs. That made at least one in seven consecutive games and broke the American League record held jointly by Ken Williams of the 1922 St Louis Browns, Lou Gehrig of the 1931 Yankees, Roy Sievers of the 1957 Washington Senators, Roger Maris of the 1961 Yankees and Reggie Jackson of the 1976 Orioles. Home runs in two more successive games would surpass the National League record. Mattingly hit a homer in game eight, but failed to get one in his ninth game, so he remains tied with Dale Long of the 1956 Pittsburgh Pirates.

Mattingly's scorching performance was even more remarkable since he concentrated more on consistent hitting than on slugging. He began playing with the Yankees in 1982, and two years later he won the American League batting title, with a .343 average. In his first three years he hit over 200 times, accumulated more than 100 RBIs and hit 20 or more home runs in each season.

A textbook hitter, he had raised his average to .327 by the end of 1987 after a disastrous beginning (.240 by the middle of June). In 20 games ending 19 July he hit 11 home runs, drove in 32 and averaged .422. Injuries hampered his play in 1990 and 1993; still, in the seven years from 1988 to 1994 he batted over .300. When he retired after the 1995 season, he held a .308 lifetime BA.

Willie 'Say Hey' Mays

Willie Howard Mays

Willie Mays does not lead in any of the columns for hitting achievements, but he is in the top five for all categories. He was a player with astonishing abilities. He hit over 40 home runs in each of six seasons, and twice he hit over 50. He drove in more than 100 runs every year for eight consecutive years (10 altogether). He hit over .300 10 times, with a .347 in 1958, and he had a lifetime average of .302. He led in slugging five times, and three times in total bases.

Mays came to the Giants in May 1951, when Leo

Durocher went looking for a player who could complement his stable of power hitters. Durocher found Mays hitting .477 for the Minnesota farm club. Mays' debut with the Giants in the majors was excruciating – he batted his first 12 times without a hit. But Durocher consoled and encouraged him, and in the next game Mays hit a home run off Warren Spahn. He hit 19 more in that first season and earned Rookie of the Year honors.

Willie played in only 34 games in his second season, spending the balance of the year and the next in military service. When he returned in 1954, he slammed 41 homers and hit at a blazing .345, with 110 RBIs – an impressive enough performance to win him his first of two MVPs. Had he played all of those two additional years, he might have won the honor of breaking Ruth's then all-time home run record, instead of ranking third, with 660.

Below left: *Legendary slugger Willie Mays with the San Francisco Giants in 1958, seven years after he joined the club.*

Below: *Mays easily outruns a throw to home plate. He had a .302 average and 3283 hits in his career.*

Willie 'Stretch' McCovey

Willie Lee McCovey

During nine of his first 13 years with the San Francisco Giants, Willie McCovey posted slugging percentages over .400 (three times over .600). But in those 13 years he had the questionable privilege of playing with a teammate regarded by a growing gallery of critics and fans as the greatest player in the game's history, the player who did everything on the field and did it exceedingly well, Willie Mays.

McCovey could have wished for more advantageous circumstances to show off his very real accomplishments. In his 15 years with San Francisco he hit 413 homers, averaging 27 per season. In 1969, the season he won the league's MVP, he hit 45 home runs, drove in 126 runs and averaged .320 in hitting.

One of the most formidable of long-ball hitters in major league history, he retired in 1980 with a total of 521 home runs (ninth in the majors). He hit 52 in his last three seasons, after he had been traded to San Diego because of doubts about his firepower. At 6'4" and 225 pounds, he was capable of pulverizing the ball any time he came to bat.

Joe 'Ducky,' 'Muscles' Medwick

Joseph Michael Medwick

Joe Medwick's career extended over 17 years (1932-48) and was divided roughly into two periods: the first eight years, when he played for the Cardinals and averaged .338; and the remaining nine, after he was traded to the Dodgers, was hit in the head by a Cardinal pitcher and never batted quite as well again. Recognized as the National League's best right-handed hitter in the 1930s, he batted over .300 during his first ten years in the league. His 64 doubles were a league record in 1936, the first of three consecutive years he won the title for RBIs.

The next year, 1937, he won the triple crown, hitting .374 and collecting 31 home runs and 137 RBIs. He led the league, as well, in runs scored, hits, total bases, doubles and slugging percentage.

A tenacious competitor, he won a reputation for hitting 'bad balls' well outside the strike zone. His aggressive approach to playing was vividly demonstrated in game seven of the 1934 World Series, when he slid into Detroit third baseman Marv Owen and the next inning was ejected by the Commissioner when fans began to threaten him. He retired with a lifetime .324 average.

Above: *Willie McCovey.*

Right: *Joe Medwick won the triple crown.*

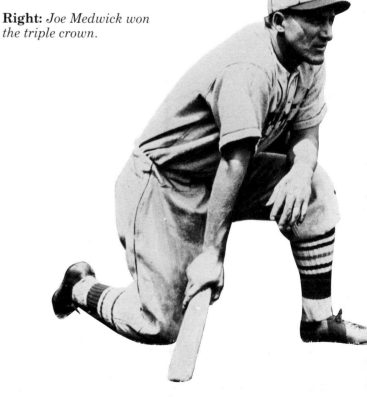

Johnny 'The Big Cat' Mize

John Robert Mize

Johnny Mize hit over .300 in his first nine years. He batted in over 100 runs in eight of his first 10 years. And from 1936 to 1948 he averaged almost 30 home runs per season. It didn't hurt that he played for two of the best teams in the history of baseball, the 1930s Cardinals and the 1950s Yankees.

With the Cardinals, in 1939, he won the league batting title by hitting .349. He also had the most home runs in the league that year, with 28, but he missed receiving the Triple Crown by accounting for only 108 RBIs, 20 fewer than the winner's. The next year he won only RBI and home run titles, losing in the hitting race, with a .314 average.

He was dubbed 'Big Cat' by a sportswriter early in his career, for he had already acquired a reputation for unusual quickness at the plate, unusual especially for a man of 6'2" and 215 pounds. During his last five years he pinch hit for the Yankees, occasionally standing in to field first base and often drawing on his vast knowledge of pitchers to help coach the younger batters.

Joe Morgan

Joseph Leonard Morgan

Left: *Second baseman Joe Morgan helped fuel the Cincinnati Reds' Big Red Machine of the 1970s that won two consecutive World Championships.*

Below: *Morgan won back-to-back MVP awards in 1975-76 and scored 1650 runs and stole 689 bases lifetime.*

When Cincinnati dominated the game in the middle 1970s, with five division titles, three pennants and two World Championships, Joe Morgan time and again took his place among the best in fielding, baserunning and hitting. He was the second National Leaguer in history to win consecutive MVP awards.

A compact 5′ 7″, 155 pounds, he was a formidable line-drive hitter who totalled over 20 home runs four times (26 in 1973 and 27 in 1976), and his 11 triples in 1971 were best in the league. He was the league's first player to hit 25 or more homers and steal at least 60 bases in the same season.

Eight times he scored 100 or more runs, including six successive years; and twice he batted over .300 – .327 in 1975 and .320 in 1976, the year he drove in 111 runs. Sparky Anderson, the Cincinnati manager in the 1970s, said he could count on Morgan to do whatever was necessary to win games. In the famous 1975 World Series with the Red Sox, Morgan was, fittingly, responsible for the winning single in game seven.

Eddie Murray

Eddie Clarence Murray

To finish a season hitting .305, with 84 RBIs and 17 home runs, and still get the blame for a team's abysmal performance would test the patience of the most stoic player. In 1986 Eddie Murray, limited by a series of injuries to 137 games, led the Orioles offensively in most categories, yet he often played to jeering fans and an accusing team owner.

Respected for his defensive consistency, as much as his batting, Murray was Rookie of the Year in 1977, the year he joined Baltimore. In 1981, the strike-shortened season, he led the league in RBIs. Two years later, he was a leader in the Orioles' World Series assault

Below: *Eddie Murray got his 3000th hit in 1995 with the Indians.*

Right: *Murray is the only player to hit homers left-handed and right-handed in a single game.*

against a talent-laden Philadelphia Phillies team. After losing the first game to the Phillies, Baltimore swept the next four.

Murray switched to the National League from 1989 through 1993 (the Dodgers from 1989 through 1991 and then the Mets in 1992-93) before going to Cleveland. Playing for a resurgent Indians club in 1995, he began to receive celebrity acclaim when he tallied his 3000th hit in June to become a member of one of the game's most select fraternities. After moving to Baltimore in July 1996, he hit his 500th home run; only two other players (Hank Aaron and Willie Mays) had ever rang up both 3000 hits and 500 home runs in a major league career.

Stan 'The Man' Musial

Stanley Frank Musial

Above: *Stan Musial scores his 30th homer of 1954.*

Right: *Musial totaled 3630 hits and 475 homers.*

Near the top of the list of best hitters for most fans would be Stan the Man Musial. Musial did not begin his hitting career modestly; he played only 12 games in his first year with the St Louis Cardinals (1941), but his performance of .426 commanded an encore. The next year he played in 140 games, and his .315 average was the third lowest mark he would have during the next 16 seasons, during which he averaged .341.

Musial stayed with the Cardinals all 24 years of his stellar career, during which he etched enough hitting records for a whole team: His 3630 lifetime hits are exceeded only by the 3771 of Hank Aaron, the 4191 of Ty Cobb and whatever Pete Rose's final tally will be. He holds second place for doubles (725) behind Tris Speaker's 793. He won seven batting titles, led the league six times in total hits, eight times in doubles, five times in triples, six times in slugging and six times in total bases.

Musial was fortunate to have few disruptions during his tenure. He lost only one year to World War II and rarely missed playing because of injury (only 24 games between 1943 and 1956). Much of his dependability, however, must be attributed to the way he approached the game and to his attitude toward himself. Admitting that he was never satisfied with a single hit in a game, he always worked for the next one. Musial had the steadiness of a skilled artisan and the manner of a true patrician.

66

Tony Oliva

Antonio Pedro Oliva

One of the last Cuban players to leave the island after Fidel Castro became premier, Tony Oliva's first two years in the major leagues in the United States provided ample explanation of why the Cuban government was so miffed by his departure. In his first year, with the Twins, Oliva became the first rookie in major league history to win the batting title. His batting average was .323 (with 217 hits – best in the league). In addition, he hit 32 home runs and 43 doubles.

To dispel any suspicions of beginner's luck, he won again the next year, batting .321, collecting 40 doubles, 98 RBIs and 185 hits. With his exceptional ability to hit equally well either right- or left-handed pitchers, he was always feared at the plate. One of his unusual talents was to connect for a line drive even on a pitch-out.

Beset with one serious weakness – bad knees – he was forced into premature retirement in 1976, after sitting out all but 10 games in 1972 and playing as designated hitter for the next three years. Much of the time he played in pain. He finished his career with a .306 lifetime average, after hitting over .300 seven times, leading the league in number of hits in five seasons and winning the batting title three times.

Above: *Tony Oliva, first to win the batting title as a rookie.*

Below: *Mel Ott (right) played for the Giants.*

Opposite: *Tony Oliva.*

Mel 'Master Melvin' Ott

Melvin Thomas Ott

Of the 511 home runs Mel Ott hit in his 22 years with the Giants, only 188 were made outside the Polo Grounds, where he took advantage of the 257-foot rightfield wall. Nevertheless, he became the first National League player to hit 500 homers, a record that stood until Willie Mays exceeded it in 1966.

At the age of 15 Ottie came to New York from Louisiana and impressed John McGraw. The manager shepherded him through his first two seasons, after which he became a regular in the line-up at the age of 19. He played with few interruptions for the next 17 years, finishing with a respectable .304 lifetime average.

In his first full year he hit 18 homers, but he received little attention because of all the noise from Yankee Stadium, where Babe Ruth was clouting his record 60. Two years later Ott unloaded for 42 home runs, and in 14 of his next 16 seasons he hit 20 or more homers per season. He led the league six times in home runs.

Dave 'Cobra' Parker

David Gene Parker

With the physique of a lumberjack, 6′ 5″, 225-pound Dave Parker intimidated pitchers ever since he began playing for Pittsburgh in 1973. Pittsburgh fans were still grieving over the loss of Roberto Clemente, killed in a plane crash in December 1972, when Parker was thrust into his position in right field and set about to fill the enormous vacancy.

His hitting during his first two years was not impressive (.288 and .282), but he became a recognized power-hitter in 1975, when he led the league in slugging and batted .308. Two years later, 1977, he hit enough to win the National League batting title, with .338. His 215 hits and 44 doubles were also best in the league that year. In 1978 he won his second batting crown, hitting .334, and for the second time he was first in the league in slugging percentage. Parker joined the Reds in the mid-1980s, hitting 26 homers in 1987.

Using his size advantageously, he could be lethal at the plate. He hit line drives off the outfield wall with no more than six-foot trajectories.

Parker spent his last four years in the American League. When he retired in 1991, he had swatted 339 homers and compiled an enviable .290 lifetime average over 19 years.

Above: *Dave Parker led the NL in slugging percentage with .541 in 1975.*

Below: *Parker moved to the Reds in the mid-1980s.*

Opposite: *Parker joined the Pirates in 1973.*

Kirby Puckett

Kirby Puckett

When he heard that the managers of the thrift department for the Twins had decided to trade their blue-ribbon reliever Rick Aguillera, Kirby Puckett carried out his own miniature tirade on the pretext that the team, in last place at the time, was throwing away its chances to be a contender. Even though the trade occurred just before mid-season, Puckett was still optimistic and this thoughts were for the team.

By the end of August 1995 the Twins had the worst record in the majors (36-66 and 32 games behind division leader Cleveland), but not because Puckett wasn't pulling his share of the load. He was batting .315 – not in the top ten but still at about the pace he maintained in his 11 years with Minnesota.

In the 1991 ALCS Puckett batted .429, hit two

Above: *The Twins' 1984 Rookie of the Year, Kirby Puckett.*

Opposite: *Puckett took the Twins to the WS title in 1987 and 1991.*

homers and drove in six in a swift 4-1 elimination of Toronto. During the Series against the Braves he swatted two more home runs and collected four more RBIs, to help bring the championship to the Twins (Puckett had also helped them win it in 1987). The next year he averaged .329, hit 19 homers and finished with 110 RBIs. His 210 total hits was best in the majors.

At the age of 34 he should have had many more years in baseball, but glaucoma forced his retirement at the beginning of the 1996 season.

Tim Raines

Timothy Raines

In the 1987 All-Star game, third longest in history (13 innings), the only player who was able to unravel the mysteries of what turned out to be a night for pitchers (score 0-0 after 12 innings) was Montreal's Tim Raines. Although he didn't enter the game until the seventh inning, he had three of the NL's eight hits – the last one a triple to drive in the winning run.

Endowed with blazing running speed (9.2 seconds in the 100-yard dash), Raines stole 70 or more bases in each of his first five years, a major league record. In the 1986 season he managed to thrust himself into scoring position 74 times in the first 79 games he played. In all he scored 91 runs in 1986, while batting .334, best in the league. Not all of his scoring threats were a result of his speed, to be sure; through the 1985 and 1986 seasons Raines ranked in the league's top ten for extra-base hitting. His .330 in 1987 was fourth best in the league.

After 14 years at Montreal, Raines went to the White Sox in 1991. He batted .306 and hit 16 home runs in 1993, his best year for Chicago. Through 1996 he remained among the league's best in lifetime average for players with careers of 16 years minimum. Raines joined the Yankees in 1996 where he had only 200 at-bats, but still hit 9 home runs and drove in 33.

Opposite top: *Montreal Expos speedster Tim Raines led the NL in batting percentage in 1986 with .334, while scoring 91 runs.*

Above, left and right: *Raines moved to the Chicago White Sox in 1991, batting .306 and hitting 16 home runs in 1993.*

Jim Rice

James Edward Rice

Tris Speaker, Ted Williams, Carl Yastrzemski – all Red Sox outfielders who hit the ball long, hard and often. Equalling and occasionally surpassing the standards of such a roster of slugging outfielders was Jim Rice. In his first five years in Boston (1975-79), on average he led the league in home runs, RBIs, slugging and total hits; and he ranked second in triples and tied for third in batting average.

In 1978, a monumental season for Rice, he became the third player in league history, after Mickey Mantle and Sam Crawford, to lead in both home runs (46) and triples (15). That year he also accumulated 406 total bases, the most since DiMaggio's 418 in 1937. He totalled 1000 hits early in his seventh season, more quickly than any other player from 1974-80.

After nearly a decade of disappointing hitting, Rice performed more characteristically in the 1986 season, with a .324 batting average (fifth best in the league) and 110 RBIs (fourth best).

Many Boston fans were sad and some were angry when Rice complained about his treatment by the city and the ballclub upon retiring in 1989. But Rice's exceptional talent and performance (382 home runs, .298 lifetime average) will keep him secure among Red Sox favorites for years.

Below: *Jim Rice played his entire career with the Boston Red Sox (1974-86).*

Opposite: *Rice became the third player to lead the AL in both HRs (46) and triples (15), in 1978.*

Cal Ripken, Jr

Calvin Edwin Ripken, Jr

Above: *Cal Ripken broke Lou Gehrig's consecutive games record of 2130 in 1995.*

Opposite: *Rookie of the Year in 1982, Ripken was MVP in 1983 and 1991.*

In the nineties, while major league baseball tries to survive once more the taint of excess that only money can engender, at least one player still emblemizes some of the old-time standards which have given meaning to superlatives in measuring performance. Cal Ripken has not hit many measured home runs. He is not listed among the leaders in total hits, nor in any of the extra-base categories, nor in slugging or even hitting average from 1990 through 1995. By the end of 1995, however, in his 15th season (all with the Orioles) he ranked 6th among active players for lifetime homers, 4th in RBIs, 7th in doubles, 9th in hits and 11th in total runs. His judges named him MVP in 1983 (his third year in the majors) and again in 1991.

Ripken's secret to achieving such rank among the best hitters still playing is no mystery at all, but has become his trademark: hard work and durability. His steadiness has led him to the smashing of one of the game's seemingly unassailable records – Gehrig's 2130 consecutive games. He played in the record-breaking game at Camden Yards on 6 September 1995 – an incredible two thousand one hundred and thirty one games in 13-plus consecutive seasons. He was just as durable in 1996 with 635 at-bats, 26 homers and 102 RBIs.

Frank Robinson

Frank Robinson

Honors as the first black manager in the major leagues and the only player to win MVP in both leagues should not distract fans from Frank Robinson's achievements as a hitter of the first rank. Considered one of the best, if not the *best*, hitter in the history of the Cincinnati franchise, where he played his first 10 years, he averaged 34 home runs, over 90 RBIs and over .300 in hitting for the Reds. In 1961, his sixth year with the team, he hit at a .323 clip, with 37 homers and 124 RBIs, and he led the league in slugging for the second of three consecutive years, with a mark of .611.

Cincinnati dealt him to the Orioles in 1966, when he was 30 years old and considered to be losing his vitality. It was no secret, as well, that he had failed to endear himself to Cincinnati fans by always turning the other cheek – just as Jackie Robinson had also behaved in Brooklyn, on instructions from Branch Rickey.

In his first year at Baltimore Frank, despite his 'fatigue', he won the Triple Crown in the American League by notching 49 homers, 122 RBIs and .316 average, thereby helping Baltimore to win its first pennant. Although he hit over .300 in nine seasons, he finished with a lifetime .294 average. But only Hank Aaron, Babe Ruth and Willie Mays have hit more than his 586 home runs.

Above: *Oriole Frank Robinson rounds the bases.*

Below: *Robinson in 1966.*

Opposite: *The Dodgers' great Jackie Robinson. In his 10 years in the majors he compiled a .311 average.*

Jackie Robinson

Jack Roosevelt Robinson

Of all the numbers to distinguish Jackie Robinson, the one probably most overlooked is the fact that he played for the relatively brief period of 10 years. But during those 10 years he became legendary. He played all 10 excelling in every assignment – hitting, fielding (at second base) and base running (he stole home 19 times in his career).

More a clutch hitter than a slugger, he hit .311 as a lifetime average, with six of his 10 years over .300. In his third and most dazzling year, 1949, he won the batting title: He averaged .342, drove in 124 runs, had 203 hits and led in stolen bases: Not surprisingly, he was also voted the league's Most Valuable Player. The year before he retired he was a force in the Dodgers' defeating the Yankees for the World Championship. But his most brilliant single-game performance came at the end of the 1951 season, when he saved a tie for first place with the hated Giants by diving to snare a blazing two-out, bases-loaded line drive in the twelfth inning and then smashing a home run to win the game in the fourteenth.

Unmistakably, his most durable legacy was his resolute will to perform as a ball player and not allow himself to be deterred by the disgraceful behaviour of many fans, writers, other players and managers. His citation in the Hall of Fame omits these credentials.

Pete 'Charlie Hustle' Rose

Peter Edward Rose

Pete Rose's first two seasons did not bode well. The man who later broke Ty Cobb's record of 4191 career hits on 11 September 1985 batted only .273 in his first season. Were it not for his persistence about being played, Cincinnati Manager Fred Hutchinson would probably have kept him on the bench. Rose got his chance in the exhibition season of 1963, but he began to have serious doubts about his ability to cope with major-league pitching after he dropped to .269 in his second year.

In the spring of his third year the aptly nicknamed 'Charlie Hustle' characteristically worked hard to improve his hitting stroke and raised his average to .312. He continued to hit over .300 for the next eight years (1965-73) and for 15 of the next 17 years. He holds a record as the player to hit over 200 times the most seasons (10), and he led the league in hits six times and in doubles four times. In the summer of 1978 he tied the National League record of hitting safely in 44 consecutive games. The following season he was playing for the Phillies.

Rose was not a natural, but what he did not have in raw ability he acquired through work and the will to excel. In the mid-1970s he was a conspicuous force for a Cincinnati team that won four pennants and two World Series.

His lifetime numbers of 160 home runs, .409 slugging and .303 hitting pale alongside his 4256 total hits – 1000 more than the total collected by any active player (Dave Winfield, 3088) through 1994.

Al 'Flip' Rosen

Albert Leonard Rosen

He played only seven full seasons in a 10-year career (1947-56), all of them with Cleveland; but in three of those seven years he hit above .300, four times he had a slugging percentage over .500 and in all but one season he hit over 20 home runs. His performance for the Indians in 1953 was impressive enough to win him the distinction of being the first player to be chosen league MVP unanimously by all 24 voters.

His 1953 season has been judged the best ever for a third baseman. His fielding was brilliant, and his hitting almost won him the triple crown, but on the last day of the season in his last at-bat his sluggish running denied him a single, and Mickey Vernon, playing for Washington, won the batting title. Flip finished that year with 43 home runs, 145 RBIs and a .336 average.

Rosen had other outstanding hitting years: He hit 37 homers in 1950 and won the league title, and in 1952 his 105 RBIs were best in the American League. Forced to retire after the 1956 season because of back problems, he finished with a career total of 192 home runs and a .285 lifetime average.

Edd 'Eddie' Roush

Edd J Roush

Edd Roush's summary assessment of the decision by some White Sox players to give away the 1919 World Series was that it wasn't necessary – Cincinnati would have won anyway. And Roush named himself as one of the biggest reasons why the Reds were the better team. Never one to underrate himself, Edd became one of the few players in history to sit out an entire season on principle, when Giant manager John McGraw refused to pay Roush's price for the 1930 season.

His numbers attest to his status as a hitter. In 1917, the year he joined Cincinnati, he won the league batting crown with a .341 average. He led the league also in 1919, hitting .321. In his nine complete seasons at Cincinnati (1917-26) he hit at a sizzling pace: .341, .333, .321, .339, .352, .351, .348, .339 and .323. His lifetime average was .323.

Although he didn't hit many home runs (67 in 18 years of playing in the majors), he did hit 329 lifetime doubles and 183 triples. In defense of his homer production he explained that he concentrated only on meeting the ball sharply. His home runs came mainly when outfielders stumbled and fell while chasing the elusive ball.

Above: *Edd Roush set for a bunt.*

Babe 'The Sultan of Swat,' 'The Bambino' Ruth

George Herman Ruth

It took 34 years for someone to break his single-season home run record of 60. His lifetime slugging average of .690 may stand forever. More than half a century after his retirement in the spring of 1935, he remains a colossus in myth and achievement.

Babe Ruth hit his benchmark 60 home runs in 1927, but that year was not his best hitting year. In 1921 he hit 59 homers, setting a new one-season record for the third year in a row. He tallied, as well, that year 44 doubles and 16 triples, drove in 171 runs and scored 177. He batted .378 and posted a slugging percentage of .846. Ted Williams alone has excelled that percentage, with .900 in 1952 and .901 in 1953.

He had all the necessary attributes for home run hitting – cat-like reflexes, exceptional vision, impeccable timing and enormous upper-body strength. His repu-tation is synonymous with home run slugging: He either led the league in home runs or tied for first place 12 times, collecting over 50 homers per season in four separate seasons. But he was respected, as well, for his consistent hitting. He batted over .370 six times, his best, .393, coming in 1923. His career average was .342.

Ruth's personal popularity was so strong among fans that he is cited as the player who rescued the game after millions became disillusioned when the White Sox scandal became public in 1920. He not only played well and hard; he also played with a flourish – and obviously had fun doing it.

Opposite top: *Babe Ruth pegs another homer for the Yankees in 1930.*   **Opposite:** *Ruth hits his 60th home run, 30 September 1927.*

Ryne Sandberg

Ryne Dee Sandberg

Ryne Sandberg went to the Cubs in 1982, after playing his first season with the Phillies. His first two years with Chicago gave no indication of any exceptional hitting talent, as he batted .271 and .261, with slugging percentages of .372 and .351. In 1984, however, he helped ignite an inert Cubs offense, and the Cubs hosted the first World Series in Wrigley Field in almost 40 years. The Cubs lost to the Padres, but Sandberg hit .368 with two doubles for the Series.

Sandberg's batting percentage in 1984 jumped 44 points over the previous year, to .314. His home run production more than doubled, from 8 to 19. He collected 200 hits and 114 runs (league best), his 19 triples were best in the league, his slugging percentage jumped to .520 and he drove in 84 runs. He won league MVP that year.

Sandberg had three more years hitting above .300 in the 1990s (.306 in 1990, .304 in 1992, and .309 in 1993); but his most impressive performance was in home runs, with an average of 25 from 1990 through 1993. After a year of retirement he returned in 1996, and added 25 more homers to his lifetime total (270) and batted in 91 runs.

Ron Santo

Ronald Edward Santo

Opposite top: *Ryne Sandberg of the Chicago Cubs.*

Opposite bottom: *Sandberg's hitting led the Cubs to the National League championship in 1984. He recorded a .520 slugging percentage, with 84 RBIs that year.*

Right: *Ron Santo, a Chicago Cub from 1960 to 1973, lines a single to centerfield, 4 July 1966, to extend his hitting streak to 26 consecutive games.*

Below: *Santo smacked 342 home runs during his major league career.*

In 11 of his 14 seasons with the Cubs (1960-73) Ron Santo hit 20 or more home runs. Four times he hit 30 or more (high of 33 in 1965). His 342 lifetime total ranks him among the 40 best home run hitters in major league history. In his best hitting year, 1964, he hit 30 homers, drove in 114 runs and batted .313, while slugging at a rate of .564. During 1964-67 he averaged 31 home runs, 102 RBIs and had over .530 in slugging percentage and .302 in hitting.

Santo often batted first in sequence before Billy Williams and Ernie Banks, yet his RBI statistics were not appreciably lower than theirs on average (Santo 96, Williams 96, Banks 105). Nonetheless, Cubs manager Durocher complained that Santo was unable to drive in runs in the clutch.

At the end of the 1973 seasons, a relatively uninspired year when he hit 20 homers, drove in 77 runs and batted .267, Santo was 34 years old and had played for the Cubs all of his 14 years. When the Cubs raised the possibility of trading Santo for two pitchers, the third baseman became the first major leaguer to exercise the option of rejecting a trade, explaining that for personal reasons he preferred to remain in Chicago. The result of this decision was that he played his last season in the Windy City. But he did not finish with the Cubs. He played, instead, in Comiskey Park, for the White Sox.

Mike Schmidt

Michael Jack Schmidt

In a single 10-inning game on 17 April 1976 Philadelphia Phillies third baseman Mike Schmidt accomplished what would satisfy many batters in a month's playing. He hit home runs in four successive times at bat and tallied 17 total bases. He later hit home runs in the next two games to tie records for homers in two and three consecutive games.

A perennial selection to the All-Star team, he was consistently a contender for the National League home run crown. His 36 homers were best in the league in 1974, and he finished in first place again in 1975 and 1976 with 38. Again, in 1977, he hit 38. He totalled 44 in 1979 and won the crown again in 1980 with 48. He reached 500 on 18 April 1987 in Pittsburgh.

Schmidt was the difference for the Phillies when they won the 1980 World Series. Only twice before had they been World Champion contenders, and both times they had lost ignominiously, having won only one game against the Red Sox in 1915 and having lost in four straight to the Yankees in 1950.

Schmidt retired in 1989, having played for the Phillies for 18 years, and was inducted into the Hall of Fame in 1995. He finished with a lifetime total of 548 home runs and an eye-popping .527 slugging percentage.

Joe Sewell

Joseph Wheeler Sewell

Joe Sewell's entrance into the major leagues came dramatically: he was called from the minors to take the place of Cleveland shortstop Ray Chapman, the only player to die from injuries sustained in a major league game. Chapman had received a skull fracture from a pitch by Yankee pitcher Carl Mays on 16 August 1920 and died the next day. Sewell proved an able stand-in and helped the Indians win the pennant.

Refusing to waste opportunities at the plate, Sewell won a reputation for being the most difficult man to strike out in baseball history. In 1925 he was fooled only four times in 672 at-bats, and in 1932 he batted 559 times and struck out in only three of them. In all of his 14 major league years he fanned only 114 times in 7132 trips to the plate, averaging approximately one strike-out every 14 games.

His extraordinary hitting eye and timing resulted in exceptional hitting numbers as well. A .312 lifetime hitter, he hit over .300 in a season 10 times, and in 1923 and 1924 he batted in over 100 runs. His most impressive hitting season was 1923, when he hit 41 doubles, 10 triples, four home runs and averaged .353.

Opposite: *Mike Schmidt of the Philadelphia Phillies hit 548 career home runs. Named National League MVP in both 1980 and 1981, he contributed to Philadelphia's 1980 World Series championship.*

Right: *Joe Sewell finished his career with the Yankees, but played for Cleveland from 1920 to 1930 alongside his brother Luke. Pitchers rarely whiffed Joe, who struck out only 114 times in 7132 at-bats.*

Above left and above: *Schmidt led the NL in home runs in 1974-76, and 1980.*

Below: *George Sisler*

Opposite top: *Enos Slaughter of the Cardinals.*

Opposite bottom: *Slaughter as a NY Yankee in the late 1950s.*

George 'Gorgeous George' Sisler

George Harold Sisler

In all but one of his last seven seasons George Sisler batted over .300, but his average for those seven years was only .319, not 'serious hitting' according to his standards. He retired after 15 seasons, all but the last three with the St Louis Browns. He retired only because his vision had been impaired by a chronic sinus infection which, in fact, had earlier forced him to miss the entire 1923 season.

During the eight years before his 1923 leave of absence he averaged .354, including .407 in 1920 and .420 in 1922. Even these extraordinary numbers won him little recognition at a time when Rogers Hornsby was receiving most of the accolades for hitting. Unlike Hornsby, however, Sisler shied away from publicity.

In his 15 years Sisler won the league batting title twice and set the league record for consecutive-game hitting at 41, in 1922, a mark that remained unsurpassed for almost 20 years, until DiMaggio raised it to 56 in 1941. In 1920 he hit 257 times, still a major league record. His lifetime batting average of .340 ranks him among the elite hitters in history.

Enos 'Country' Slaughter

Enos Bradsher Slaughter

If hustle is one of the essential qualifications for excellence in baseball, then Enos Slaughter can take his place alongside such other driven competitors as Pete Rose, Jackie Robinson and Frankie Frisch. Characteristic of his relentless pursuit was his tie-breaking score from first base in the eighth inning of game seven to enable the Cardinals to win the 1946 World Series against the Red Sox. Shortstop Johnny Pesky 'blinked' before relaying the ball home, and Slaughter scored.

A member of the Cardinals' 'Gashouse Gang' of the 1930s, Slaughter batted over .300 in 10 of his 19 years in the major leagues, including a .304 (in 77 games as a pinch hitter) the year before he retired at the age of 43. His best hitting average was .336 in 1949. Three times he drove in more than 100 runs per season. In 1946, after three years in the service, he was first in the majors, with 130 runs. In nine seasons he had over 150 hits per season, leading the league in 1942 with 188. Although he was never a threat as a home run hitter, he tallied a respectable 413 doubles and 148 triples. His lifetime average, after 19 years of feverish, abandoned playing, was .300.

Duke 'The Silver Fox' Snider

Edwin Donald Snider

The team that most often carried the National League standard against the Yankees in the World Series during the 1950s was the Brooklyn Dodgers, and the best slugger the Dodgers had in those championship games was Duke Snider. Snider's World Series home run hitting remains among the best in the history of season's finales. There was a period in the mid-1950s, in fact, when Snider fans argued that their hero was as good or better than Willie Mays or Mickey Mantle. In six Series with the Dodgers, he hit 11 homers, and twice he hit four in a single Series.

One of Roger Kahn's 'boys of summer,' he was a

fabulous home run hitter, with 40 or more a year for five consecutive years, 1953-57. In 10 of 11 years he hit 20 or more a year, and he led the league once in both homers and RBIs. In his most productive year, 1955, his hitting average was .309, he slammed 42 homers, he had 136 RBIs and the Dodgers finally beat the Yankees in the World Series.

After the Dodgers left New York in 1958, the Duke had two more years of outstanding hitting, with .312 and .308 averages, but his home run total dropped from the 23 he had hit in his last year at Ebbets Field (1957) to 6 in his first season in Los Angeles.

Tris 'The Grey Eagle,' 'Spoke' Speaker

Tristram E Speaker

The only time Ty Cobb did not win the American League batting title in the years between 1907 and 1919 was 1916, when Tris Speaker led with a .386 average. By any standard Speaker's hitting records are superlative, but his authority at the plate was usually overlooked because his playing years (1907-1928) were almost identical to Cobb's (1905-1928).

Speaker hit over .300 in 18 of his 22 years, and he hit over .370 six times. He led the league in doubles eight times, and he amassed a lifetime total of 793 two-baggers. His 3515 total hits places him fifth on the all-time list, and his lofty .344 lifetime average is the seventh highest in history.

His hitting helped the Red Sox win the World Series in 1912, when he batted .383. In 1920, while playing and managing for Cleveland, he hit .388 for the season and .320 in the Series, to help the Indians beat the Dodgers for the World Championship.

He resigned as manager of Cleveland at the end of the 1926 season when stories began circulating that he and Ty Cobb had fixed games. By the next season all such charges had been dropped, and Speaker returned to play for Washington for a year, and then for one final season with Philadelphia.

Opposite: *Brooklyn Dodger Duke Snider wallops his second home run in the sixth game of the 1952 World Series. 'The Silver Fox' hit a total of 11 home runs in six Series.*

Right: *Tris Speaker played outstanding baseball in the 1912 and 1920 World Series, batting .383 and .320, respectively.*

Willie 'Pops' Stargell

Wilver Dornel Stargell

Willie Stargell never did win a batting title for his hitting average. His best was .315, in 1966, and in all his years with the Pirates he had only three seasons over .300. But he was twice winner of the home run crown. His career strikeout record would suggest that at least one reason why he was unable to maintain a high hitting average was his intention to pulverize the ball each time he went to the plate.

Fifteen times he hit 20 or more home runs per season, with highs of 48 in 1971 and 44 in 1973. He drove in more than 100 runs five times, and over 90 four other times. But in his two best home run and RBI years he did not have a high enough average to win league MVP. In 1979, however, he tied with batting leader Keith Hernandez for National League MVP when, at the age of 38, he managed 32 homers, 82 RBIs and an average of .281. That year he was also named MVP in the National League championship series with Cincinnati, and his .400 hitting won him MVP for the 1979 World Series.

Willie Starge 8

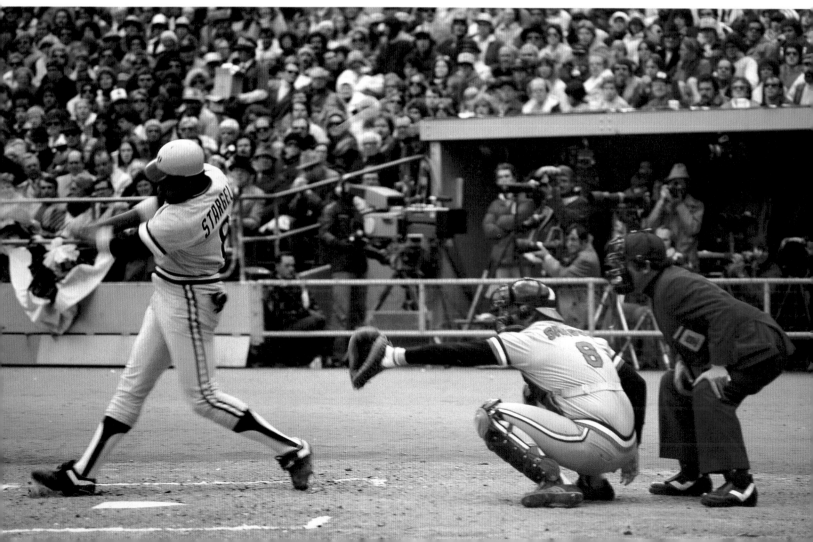

Bill 'Memphis Bill' Terry

William Harold Terry

Bill Terry made no apology for his contention that he was the best hitter in baseball during his playing years – 1923-36 – all of them with the Giants. Terry may have lacked modesty when he began playing for John McGraw, but he was certainly not deficient in batting savvy. Touted as the premier first baseman in National League history, he balanced superior defensive play with consistent hitting. Beginning in 1927, he hit over .300 for 10 consecutive years, his best production coming in 1930, when he became only the second and last player (after Rogers Hornsby) in National League history to go over .400, with a .401.

He stands second to Hornsby's league-leading lifetime average (.358), with a mark of .341. The same year that he went over .400 he tied the league record for total hits, with 241. He hit over 200 six times, and from 1927-32 he collected more than 100 RBIs.

McGraw was never able to abide Terry's arrogance, but prudence dictated that McGraw name his first baseman as the choice to succeed him as manager of the Giants. McGraw's judgment was sound: as player-manager Terry won three pennants over the next six years, as well as the World Series in 1933.

Opposite: *Willie Stargell.*

Above and below: *Bill Terry.*

Frank Thomas

Frank Edward Thomas

Just about the time fans were beginning to reminisce about all the great hitters of decades past, along comes one who has all the markings of a pedigreed giant at the plate. In his first five years playing in the majors (all with the White Sox), Frank Thomas has become the most dominant hitter in the league. Discounting his first season, when he played only 60 games, and the inconclusive 1994 numbers, his performances are in the stratosphere range of all-time great hitters. And he is only 27 years old.

After his first full season (1991) his hitting average

and slugging percentage were indicators that his talent was prodigious; but skeptics justifiably cautioned that it was still too early. His numbers, though, were sensational, including 32 homers and an on-base percentage (perhaps most telling of all the hitting categories) that was league best at .453.

Confounding his doubters, Thomas carried on at an even more feverish pace in his third and fourth years (1992-93). In 1993 the White Sox won the division title, their first crown since 1959 when they won the pennant. It was no coincidence that Thomas hit 41 HRs,

Above: *The top young slugger in baseball today, Frank Thomas has an exceptionally good eye at the plate.*

Above right and right: *In 1993 Thomas took the White Sox to their first division title since 1959. He was MVP in 1992 and 1993.*

batted in 128 runs and finished the year with a .601 slugging percentage. In the series against Toronto he hit at a .353 clip, but the Blue Jays prevailed in six.

His performance in 1992-93 was exceptional enough to win him MVP both times. His pace was no less torrid in 1996: second best in the majors in batting (.348), eighth in league home runs (40), and sixth in slugging (.625). His prospects for joining the ranks of the game's elite corps of hitters are becoming more persuasive every additional year he plays.

Alan Trammell

Alan Stuart Trammell

Alan Trammell joined the Detroit Tigers in 1977. Early in his career it became apparent that he was not only a brilliant shortstop but also an extraordinary hitter. He averaged .268 in his second year, and by 1980 he had a batting average of .300.

His best year was also the Tigers' best year in recent memory: 1984. That year the team won 104 games and, eventually, the World Championship. Trammell (who has four Gold Glove Awards) was spectacular in his defensive play, and his .314 batting average set a standard for the team.

He ended the year in a blaze of glory in the World Series against the San Diego Padres. His nine hits –

two of them homers – in 20 at-bats gave him an impressive .450 average. In all, he scored five runs and batted in six. Detroit took the Series 4-1, and Trammell was named the Series MVP.

In the years since, his dependability and leadership proved to be a real asset to the Tigers. In 1987 Trammell's .343 average, 105 RBIs and 28 HRs helped the Tigers overtake and defeat Toronto. In 1990 Trammell hit 14 home runs and batted .304, and in 1993 he averaged .329 with 12 homers.

After 20 extremely productive years with the Tigers, Trammell finally retired at the end of the 1996 season.

Right: *Alan Trammell, 1984 World Series MVP, with two homers and a .450 batting average, is lifted high as his Detroit Tiger teammates go haywire after capturing the World Championship, 14 October 1984.*

Honus 'The Flying Dutchman' Wagner

John Peter Wagner

Honus Wagner, one of the five original inductees into the Hall of Fame in 1936, played for Louisville in the National League from 1897-99. He then went to Pittsburgh for the balance of his career, 1900-17. Acclaimed by rival managers as the 'best all-round ballplayer who ever lived,' Wagner did not hit as low as .300 until his

Right: *Honus Wagner, 17-year veteran of the Pirates, won eight batting titles and entered the Hall of Fame in 1936.*

Below: *Wagner posted a .333 batting average in the 1909 World Series.*

seventeenth year. His average those 17 years was .339, with a high of .381 in his first year with the Pirates (1900).

Wagner won the league batting title a record eight times, and he helped the Pirates dominate the league during the century's first decade. In 1909, after winning 110 games and the National League pennant, the Pirates played the Tigers in the first World Series to extend to a full seven games. In this Series Wagner took advantage of his only opportunity to match his hitting against that of Ty Cobb. Cobb had finished the regular season hitting at a .377 pace, and Wagner at a mere .339. During the Series Cobb's average was .321, while Wagner hit .333.

He retired in 1917, still with the Pirates, at the age of 43. He had hit 3430 times, a league record for 45 years, until it was broken by Stan Musial in 1963.

Paul 'Big Poison' Waner

Paul Glee Waner

Paul Waner didn't hit below .300 until he was in his twelfth year in the majors. Beginning with the Pirates in 1926, at the age of 23, he quickly established a reputation as a dangerous hitter by batting .336 and leading the league with 22 triples. It was a sensational beginning, but it was merely prelude to more than a decade of soaring hitting numbers. He won the batting title in his second year with a .380 average, 17 triples, 237 hits and 131 RBIs – all the highest in the league. He won his second batting crown in 1934, hitting .362, and a third two years later, with a .373 mark. He remained with the Pirates for 15 of his 20 years in the majors.

Paul learned to hit by batting pieces of corncob with a broken broomstick in his time off from farm work in Oklahoma. The erratic path of the cobs enabled him to connect with most any kind of pitch he would see in the majors (including those he had trouble following because of double vision from too much drinking).

In this century only Rogers Hornsby and Bill Terry surpassed his lifetime average of .333 for National League players in 1000 games or more.

Billy Williams

Billy Leo Williams

Billy Williams was one of those ballplayers who did what he had to do quietly and reliably for 18 years, all but the last two played at Wrigley Field in Chicago. Playing for the Cubs at the time Ernie Banks was deservedly receiving accolades for his home run performances, Williams got relatively little attention.

But his modesty could not disguise his hitting achievement, and in his first year (1961) he was voted Rookie of the Year. In 1972 he led the league in hitting, with a .333 average, and batted over .300 four other times in his 18-year career, finishing with a .290 lifetime average. His home run high came in 1970, when he totalled 42. He holds twentieth place in major-league career home runs, with 426.

Recognized for his durability as well as his lightning swing, he played in 1117 consecutive games from 22 September 1963 through 2 September 1970 – at that time a National League record that earned him the title of 'Iron Man of the Chicago Cubs.'

The Cubs traded him to Oakland at the end of the 1974 season. In his first year with the A's he hit 23 homers and drove in 81 runs to help Oakland win their fifth consecutive division title.

Below: *Willie Mays greets Billy Williams as he crosses the plate after hitting the first home run of the 1964 All-Star Game.*

Opposite top: *Paul Waner.*

Opposite bottom: *Waner entered the Hall of Fame in 1952 with a .333 batting average.*

Ted 'The Splendid Splinter' Williams

Ted Williams

Ted Williams may have inadvertantly spoken for all aspiring hitters when he confessed in his rookie year, 'All I want out of life is that when I walk down the street folks will say, "There goes the greatest hitter who ever lived."' More than a quarter century after his retirement (1960), only four other players in this century have better lifetime averages for 1000 or more games played: Ty Cobb, Rogers Hornsby, Joe Jackson and Tris Speaker.

Often judged as remote by sportswriters and fans, Williams methodically went about setting standards for hitting which seem almost impossible now. He won six batting titles in 19 seasons. After hitting .327 in his rookie year he reached an astonishing .406 only two years later. His lifetime average of .344 would be an enviable single-season mark for most present-day title contenders. Batting over .350 five different years, and over .387 in his four best, he remains, through 1987, the best hitter since Rogers Hornsby.

He studied the mechanics of hitting tirelessly, but he saw no reason to discuss his technique: He just went out and hit. Characteristic of his approach to his achievement was his decision to finish the 1941 season by playing in a doubleheader with Philadelphia, despite the advice from Joe Cronin to stay out of the games and protect his average of .3995. In those games he hit six of eight times he went to the plate and pushed his average up six whole points.

Hack Wilson

Lewis Robert Wilson

In 1929 the Chicago Cubs owned the most explosive aggregate of right-handed hitters in the history of baseball. Considered the home run slugger on that stellar roster (which included Rogers Hornsby, who hit .380) was Lewis 'Hack' Wilson, who had 39 home runs that season. His next year was even better, with 56 homers – still the National League record – the all-time major league RBI record of 190, as well as a .356 average.

Hack Wilson began playing for John McGraw and the Giants, but the Cubs snared him when someone in the Giants' management got careless and left him eligible for the draft. McGraw was livid, but he could only look on as Wilson began building a reputation for consistent and dangerous hitting with the Cubs, for whom he played six years.

Compact as a fireplug (5' 6" and 195 pounds), Wilson could deliver a savage swing. In his 12 years in the major leagues he hit 244 home runs and averaged a lifetime .307, numbers not particularly remarkable except when you consider that six of those years he hit fewer than 15 homers, and only five times did he average over .300. He delighted fans, but often alarmed the rest of the team by spending the night partying.

Left: *Burly Hack Wilson delivers one out of Wrigley Field.*

Below: *Wilson slugged 56 home runs and 190 RBIs in 1930.*

Opposite top: *Dave Winfield of the Yankees jumped from Big Ten baseball at Minnesota directly to the big leagues. He soon lived up to his All-Star potential, batting .308 in 1979, with a league leading 118 RBIs.*

Opposite bottom: *Pity the catcher who gets in big Dave Winfield's way at the plate. Here Winfield flies into home for a fourth inning score against the Chicago Cubs, 9 July 1975.*

Dave Winfield

David Mark Winfield

When Dave Winfield joined the Padres in 1973 he had just left the University of Minnesota, where he played basketball, football and baseball well enough to win draft positions in all three sports. He chose baseball because of the greater promise of longevity.

With no time to adjust from Big Ten competition to the National League, he was thrust into the outfield. After hitting a disappointing three home runs and batting .277 in 56 games in his rookie season, he steadily improved, and in 1977 he hit 25 homers. During the next two seasons he averaged over .300. His 118 RBIs in 1979 were the most in the league.

Winfield joined the Yankees in 1981, and became a consistent leader in at least one hitting category. In 1984, for example, he lost the batting title to fellow Yankee Don Mattingly only on the last day of the season. In his first four years with New York he totalled 390 RBIs.

His 1986 season was one of his poorest – he batted only .262, yet he hit 24 home runs and drove in 104. By the time of the All-Star break in 1987, he ranked in the top ten in the American League in four hitting categories: RBIs, on-base percentage, runs scored and walks. By season's end, Winfield had a .275 batting average, 97 RBIs, and 27 homers.

Moving from Minnesota to Cleveland in 1995, he helped the Indians reach the World Series for the first time in 41 years. Winfield retired before the 1996 season. In his 23-year career he posted impressive lifetime numbers including 3,110 career hits.

Carl 'Yaz' Yastrzemski

Carl Michael Yastrzemski

Not since Ted Williams had Boston seen a hitter who could so electrify fans every time he came to bat. Yaz came to the Red Sox in 1961, the year after Williams' retirement, and after 23 seasons he had left almost as indelible a mark as his predecessor.

His first six years disappointed many fans because he averaged only 16 home runs per season and had a .294 average, with only two years over .300. Yastrzemski had concentrated more on consistency than distance, and he began having second thoughts about his place in Boston in 1966, when fans watched the Red Sox finish ninth and put a lot of the blame on Yaz.

The next year, 1967, Carl erupted with 44 home runs, 121 RBIs and a .326 hitting average that did much to lead Boston to its first pennant in 21 years. They did not win that title until the last game of the season, but in the final ten games Yastrzemski batted over .500, winning league MVP and the Triple Crown.

Although he averaged over .300 only six times in his career, he won two other batting titles apart from the 1967 season (1963 and 1968). He also led in hits twice, in doubles three times and in slugging percentage three times. In 1975 he batted .310 in the historic World Series with Cincinnati. He became the first American Leaguer to accumulate 3000 hits and 400 home runs before retiring, which he did in 1983.

Opposite and right: *Carl Yastrzemski, legendary Beantown batter, was a favorite with Boston fans. 'Yaz' won three separate batting titles, a 1967 MVP Award and Triple Crown, and he chalked up 3000 hits and 400 homers during his career.*

Ross 'Pep' Youngs

Ross Middlebrook Youngs

New York Giants Manager John McGraw made no secret of his feelings towards his players and, consequently, was unable to get along with very many of them. Ross Youngs, however, was one of McGraw's favorites, and he was a major reason why the Giants won pennants from 1921 to 1924.

Pep Youngs would have preferred to play for the Detroit Tigers when the Giants picked him up in 1916. Nevertheless, he batted .302 in his first full year in New York (1918) and readily won recognition both for his defensive play in right field and for his hitting.

In his second year Youngs led the league, with 31 doubles, and he finished the season with a .311 hitting average. In 1920 he was second in the race for the batting title, behind Rogers Hornsby. In 1921, the first of four successive pennant-winning years for the Giants, Youngs was a key performer in the third game of the World Series against the Yankees. He hit a double and a triple in the seventh inning in two at-bats.

The next year, 1922, he batted .331 and had an even better World Series, again played against the Yankees. He hit .375 for the Series, while his counterpart in right field for the Yankees, Babe Ruth, hit a mere .118.

Robin Yount

Robin R Yount

Few American League regular seasons have closed more dramatically in the 1980s than did the season of 1982, when the Brewers and Orioles, the first and second place teams in the East, collided in a final four-game series. Milwaukee began the series with a four-game lead, but then the Brewers lost the next three games to Baltimore before winning their final regular season game and the division title. A prominent figure in Milwaukee's season-long conquest was shortstop Robin Yount, who had put together one of the best all-around hitting performances of the decade. Yount led the league that year in hits (210), doubles (46) and slugging (.578). He scored 129 runs, hit 29 homers, drove in 114 and batted .331 – a heroic achievement that won him MVP honors. The Brewers went on to become the first major league team to recover from a two-game deficit and win the league Championship Series (against the Angels).

In the World Series, which Milwaukee lost to St Louis in seven games, Yount batted brilliantly, with three doubles, a home run and a .414 hitting average.

He became the first player in Series history to have two four-hit games.

During the late 1980s through 1993 (when he retired) Yount maintained his status as a dreaded hitter on an otherwise disappointing Milwaukee team. Even though he did not claim any more batting crowns, his home run totals were in double figures four of his last six years and his career total reached 251. A lifetime hitting average of .285 holds his place among exceptional batters.

Above: *Ross Youngs played for the New York Giants from 1917 to 1926. Youngs was either a contender for leading the league or led the league in all statistical departments year after year. He entered the Hall of Fame in 1972.*

Opposite: *The Milwaukee Brewers' Robin Yount won the American League MVP in 1982. Yount's hitting sparked the Brewers to a league championship that year, and he batted brilliantly in the World Series against St Louis.*